Centering Our Souls
Devotional Reflections
of a University President

Centering Our Souls
Devotional Reflections
of a University President

R. Kirby Godsey
President, Mercer University

MERCER
UNIVERSITY PRESS

ISBN 0-86554-985-0   MUP/H652

Centering Our Souls:
Devotional Reflections of a University President
©2005 Mercer University Press
1400 Coleman Avenue
Macon, Georgia 31207 USA
All rights reserved
Printed in the United States of America
First edition, December 2005

The paper used in this publication meets the minimum
requirements of American National Standard
for Information Sciences—Permanence of Paper
for Printed Library Materials, ANSI Z39.48-1992. ∞

Library of Congress Cataloging-in-Publication Data

Godsey, R. Kirby (Raleigh Kirby), 1936–   .
    Centering our souls : devotional reflections
of a university president / R. Kirby Godsey. — 1st ed.
        p.   cm.
    Includes bibliographical references.
    ISBN-13: 978-0-86554-985-2 (hardcover : alk. paper)
    ISBN-10: 0-86554-985-0 (hardcover : alk. paper)
    1. Christian life—Meditations.
2. Christian life—Baptist authors. I. Title.
    BV4832.3.G63 2005
    242—dc22

                                    2005020731

Contents

Preface

Most of us live scattered lives, pulled in different directions, running to stay in place. Our human journeys turn out not to be smooth sailing on calm waters from sunrise to sunset. We are more likely to be tossed about on rough seas, even finding ourselves sometimes grounded on the shoals of some strange land. Our complex lives are often not shaped by predictable plans but by unexpected events.

So, I gather these reflections as an individual who lives and works amidst complexity. These writings claim no grandiose or startling revelations. Rather, they open a window on my own spiritual sojourn as I seek to define a center for my soul. Centering provides a means of seeing through the maze of competing demands. Centering offers a measure of simplicity that can bring order and even rest in a world that seems prone toward chaos.

Our human ways are also being challenged by a world that is collapsing into a tiny microcosm. No longer are our human destinies independent or remote. More than ever in human history, our lives overlap. What happens to one of us affects all of us. Centering can become a powerful resource in a world where we live up close and personal. Centering is about learning who we are and what matters to us, and learning to respect the soul-centers of those who live so close to us. Centering should never degenerate into the defensive act of compelling others to walk where we walk, to believe what we believe, or to value precisely what we value. Centering, instead, is about defining a home base of self-understanding, about discovering an integrating factor for our own lives.

The effort to compel others by the force of our rhetoric or the tactics of fear to conform to our view of the world is the most telling evidence that we do not trust our own center. It is easy to become convinced that our beliefs are secure only if we can defeat those who have formed a different understanding of what it means to be present in the world. Therein lies the danger of evangelism, whether that evangelism be Muslim, Christian, Jewish, or the latest new orthodoxy. There is a narrow line between confessing the light by which we live, and by threat of death or damnation to compel others to concede to our truth. The frantic push to make others conform to our affirmations of faith indicates, above all else, that we have failed to achieve a centering solace within our own souls.

The addresses and homilies included here represent a broad range of expressions of my own life of devotion. Indeed, it has been the life of devout belief that has served me as a reservoir of hope in the midst of a professional life that has been fraught with challenges and high expectations. I have embraced my life of work with energy and sheer delight. But work alone cannot make us whole. We can endure the debris of daily difficulties and decisions only by cultivating the inner life so that we know that we are more than the work we do and the decisions we make. Our lives can be consumed by activity. Busyness can become a foil for facing into our own sense of meaning and purpose. I am convinced that fulfillment springs rather from bringing the life of thought and the life of devotion together. It is called centering the soul.

The audiences for these essays and addresses have been diverse. They included college students beginning their studies, congregations waiting expectantly for a word. They have been professional educators, trying to find a distinctive reason for integrating faith and learning. They have been preachers, longing to hear a word because their well of understanding seems at times like it is running dry. But, in every case, I do not speak as a person with a bag full of answers. I come as a seeker along the way, confessing my faith, hoping to reflect the light that has come to my path. My goal is to call out encouragement to others who seek a better way. We should make our journeys of belief together, seeking to find a center to hold our fractious lives together, while respecting the diverse lights by which we live.

In these writings, you will certainly encounter recurring themes. For example, in two very different contexts, I speak of the drama of dread that accompanied the encounter between Jacob and Esau. Moses' experience before the "burning bush" becomes the reference point for differing reflections on the life of faith and the life of ministry. Biblical stories can often become parables for our own human condition. These recurring themes also convey that all our affirmations of faith are tightly interwoven. Rarely does one affirmation stand alone.

In my reflections on the life of faith, you will find that I am more disciple than teacher, more learner than oracle. In these texts, I am inviting you to join me in my ongoing search for meaning.

Our understanding of ourselves, our understanding of the complex world in which we live, and our understanding of God can be enriched, I believe, as we share our human journeys, confess our faiths, and reach out in a common search to center our souls.

Children of Hope

When you and I consider our different worlds—different families, different backgrounds, different interests, different preoccupations, a few threads continue to bind us together even amidst our differences. One thread through which we are profoundly connected is that we are all children of hope. I believe that two words, more than any others, embody the power of the gospel. The words are Grace and Hope.

Today I speak of hope. The Sundays of our lives represent our reaching for hope. People find their way to sanctuaries, not because they envision death, but because they are reaching out for life. The celebration called worship is first and foremost about life and hope.

Without hope, our lives sink into deeper and deeper depression. Life is not sustained by what we know or what we have achieved or even what we have acquired. Life, at its center, is sustained by hope. Knowledge without hope leaves us empty. Power and prestige without hope leaves us bitter and angry. Wealth without hope leaves us in despair. Add hope to knowledge and we will be on the road that leads to wisdom. Add hope to power and prestige and you have the prospect for benevolence and progress. Add hope to wealth and you have the foundation for giving.

In very personal ways, we all know what it means to feel hopeless. The face of hurt and the presence of crippling and life-threatening diseases find their way into the days of all our lives. And when they do, it seems there is nowhere to go, no way beyond the uncertainty and the fear that grips us. The pain seems endless. The struggle feels useless.

The Christian faith that you and I embrace is not a faith which fails to face into the harsh realities of our lives. The Christian faith does not call us to enter a make-believe world. Our faith does speak of joy, but it is not a joy that ignores the pain.

If hope is to come alive, it must be born amidst the real and even troublesome days in which we live. Hope has to be born in a world where fear and uncertainty frequently invade our lives. I confess to being a person who knows the meaning of uncertainty. I have labored in a university when everything nailed down seemed to be coming loose. I have known ill winds, have felt the pain of crippling criticism, and have known the silence of long days and longer nights. I have walked through the valleys of uncertainty.

In our families especially, we all know what pain is like. We have watched mothers and fathers leave us and we are left to cope with life alone. We have lost husbands and wives to death and divorce, when our lives were so tightly interwoven that we did not think we could do life alone. We have struggled through great illnesses that left us exhausted emotionally and physically. Grief and turmoil, uncertainty and despair, are not realities that are remote. They belong to our ordinary lives. Only the names and faces change.

So, in real life, we need the sunrise of hope—a hope that does not ask us to pretend or make-believe. We need hope that gives us the energy and the courage to carry on. The Christian faith offers us a way of finding hope. And if we are to hear that word, we must be prepared to distinguish in our lives between the meaning of time and eternity.

Our culture loves New Year celebrations. Each year, we count the seconds as a large ball in New York City drops before a throng of people longing for new beginnings. We celebrate the New Year by making predictions and endless resolutions. Yet, as we celebrate, we have the uneasy sense that the calendar change alone will not bring hope. Hope will never be the child of time itself.

You and I are time-centered, time-conscious beings. We are consumed by time. We live by the clock, getting up by the clock, going to bed by the clock. It is time to go to work, and "quitting time." Our talk is dominated by where and when. We become possessed by the passing of time—especially as we grow older. We monitor our lives with clocks—clocks that ring school bells, clocks where we punch in and punch out. There are clocks that chime in case we are not watching. There are clocks that alarm when our sleep is too sound. Clocks blow whistles in the city at noontime. We are time-centered people. We measure our lives by the number of days we have lived. He lived to be 82. She lived to be 77. He died when he was only 54. We often measure our lives by time.

The real genius of the Christian faith is that we are invited to look at our lives from a different point of view. The religious word for that viewpoint is called eternity. But eternity is not about time or more of it. Our faith does not offer us an escape from time. It offers us a new way of thinking about our lives, a new way of seeing what it means to be here.

While we are watching the clock, our faith says to us, "Listen. Be careful. Do not define your life by time." Do not define your life by the clock. You and I are more than the days we live.

I say to people that our lives are lived between the "not-yet" and the "no-longer." There was a time when we were not yet here. There will be a time when we are here no longer. We live in between. We live between the not yet and the no longer.

If the future toward which you and I live is a future in time, we are utterly, utterly, without hope. If we live toward more time, nothing but tragedy awaits us. To the prosperous farmer, Jesus said, "This night, your soul will be required of you." The point is this: Our time will run out. Our clock will stop. When the ticking of the clock has finished for us, whether we have lived 80 years or 40 years, will not matter very much. What will matter will be how we have framed those years.

The gospel reminds us that we are more than our time. If we think of our lives only in terms of time—the clock, we are nothing more than what happens between being born and dying. Time turns out to be a pitifully empty definition for the meaning of our lives.

Jesus sets out to do nothing less than to change radically how we see our lives. If Jesus is able to change how we see our lives, he will usually have to do so despite our religion. Religion often becomes one more time-centered enterprise. Religion gets confused as being a way of getting more time, indeed, getting endless time. Bad religion. The Christian faith is not about getting more time. It is about getting more life.

Eternity, one of those giant, awesome religious words, has nothing to do with time. It is not about getting more days. This matter of looking at life from the standpoint of eternity to which Jesus introduces us is nothing less than a new way of seeing who we are and what our being here is about. Jesus says to us: "Do not measure your life by time or by time's necessities—food, clothing, and shelter."

Instead, Jesus proposes for us a new way of seeing what we are doing here. The measure of our lives is no longer how long we have lived, but how deeply we have loved. Jesus was very direct. He said it very plainly. Measure your life, he says, by how much you love God and how much you care about other people. That is a radically different way of looking at ourselves and our reason for being here.

This new way of seeing ourselves even changes the way we understand death. Death is not the end of life. Death is the end of time. If we have lived only for the gifts of time, the celebrations of time, the achievements of time, our time will be up. We can try to add a few days in the hope that the addition of days will add life. It will never happen. The extension of days will not add life. It can only delay death.

Hope will never be born simply by adding years. Hope is born when we begin to look at our years in a new way. There is a new prospect for understanding our being here. If we are to find hope, we must have the courage to see life in a new way. We learn from Jesus that hope does not rest in survival. It was clear that Jesus wanted to survive. As he rode in on that Palm Sunday, the last thing he wanted was rejection and hurt. He was not eager to give up and bear the pains of crucifixion. Rejection is never an easy experience. But the simple truth is this: Our hope does not ultimately lie in surviving. We will not. If we live only to survive, we lose. The real hope of life will not stand on the gain or the loss of time.

People don't much need a doctrine of hope. What they need is hope. Hope sometimes means walking with someone down the long and difficult road of getting well. Hope sometimes means having the courage to let go of someone who will not get well.

Only a few years ago, my friend, Pat, died from the ravages of breast cancer. Only a few hours before she died, I sat beside her, and we talked of death. I had taught her in college as a young woman. She had struggled so intensely, doing everything known to be done, undergoing every therapy, faithfully following all the regimens. The breast cancer won. Until the end, she was lucid, clearheaded and thoughtful. She and I talked about her struggle and the uneasy prospects of letting go. She said to me, "I am going to embrace death in the hope that death is a friend." Only two days later, Pat died. Hope is not always a way out. It is sometimes a way into death.

Hope is born when grace breaks down the barriers of fear. Hope offers us no glib assertion that everything is going to be alright. Hope does not take away the trouble. Hope changes the impact of trouble upon us. Hope changes the way we face that which is not alright. Hope gives us the courage to struggle. Hope gives us the strength to live and the courage to endure.

Hope does not say, "Don't worry about it. God will take care of everything." We live in a world where everything is not alright. People are abandoned. Senseless violence stretches out before us in living color. Hope searches for ways to overcome terrorism. Hope becomes a part of undoing the violence of abuse and abandonment. Hope embraces the lonely. Hope carries coats to the elderly in winter. Hope takes the homeless home. Hope builds houses for the impoverished. Hope feeds the hungry and clothes the naked. Hope forgives the hurt.

Hope is not abstract. Hope is not a vague yearning for things to get better. Hope is a decision. Hope is an action. Hope changes how we behave. Hope changes how we specifically conduct our lives. God's presence changes the character of our being here. To be Christian means to add to the gift of life, the gift of hope.

Hope is not about making it past Judgment Day. It is not even about getting to heaven and avoiding hell. Hope means finding the courage to live our years with the power and presence of God within us. Hope means that God is with us. God is in us and God is for us.

Becoming a person of hope means claiming the power of God's presence within us. Our lives are more important than time will ever reveal. We were created to love freely and to forgive without condition. As we find the courage to love and forgive, we become children of hope.

Amen.

The Long Journey to Easter

Our human journeys turn out to be passages that are broken and uneven. We course our way through the shadows and the patches of light. We experience moments of real triumph when we seem to explode with excitement. Yet, woven among those steps that bring excitement are the steps that bring uneasiness and make us dread to face another day.

The biblical story of Palm Sunday points us toward the drama of this human contradiction. The biblical drama describes Jesus as being at the center of an admiring throng, a crowd of people waving palm leaves and shouting their "Hallelujahs!" But the whole affair was twisted, based upon a misunderstanding. Jesus was a stately character but he turned out not to be the king they thought he was or wanted him to be. He knew what was waiting for him in Jerusalem even though they did not.

The Bible says Jesus moved "steadfastly toward Jerusalem." No easy journey. He loved that city, Jerusalem, yet he feared it. This was no artificial fear. It was the kind of fear that makes you shake inside, that makes you lose your appetite, that makes you dread to take another step.

Jerusalem turned out to be a dreadful place. The city not only marked the assault of his enemies, it also witnessed the rejection of his friends. It was here that Judas betrayed him, that Peter denied him. It was here that his disciples left him and fled. It was here that the last flicker of hope seemed to die.

Yet, it was here, in this very place, that the Christian church was to begin. You would have thought that Jesus would have said, "Start anywhere but Jerusalem." They were to begin here. The dreadful place is often the place where we have to begin.

We must understand this truth about our human journeys, both as individuals and as a church. We cannot begin where we are not. We tear at our hearts, and wrestle with our wills, longing to be somewhere else. But one of the important marks of a journey is where you begin, and we can only begin where we are. We can begin only with the reality of our own experience. The former secretary-general of the United Nations, Dag Hammarskjöld, said, "The longest journey is the journey inwards." We cannot go anywhere, achieve anything worthy, until we face where we are.

So, I speak of new beginnings. As private persons, most of us long from time to time for a new beginning. And our longing is really for a clean slate. We long to erase the bad choices and the hateful words we have spoken. We want to restore the broken hearts and to dry the tears. We find ourselves saying, "I wish I hadn't said that." But our journeys are not like that. Our new beginnings will have to take seriously where we are. We cannot simply wish that we were not there.

My point is that a new beginning must be built upon the realities of our old journeys. A new beginning is not a way of escaping past mistakes. We should not defend those activities that cannot be defended and explain whose words that cannot be explained. Rather, we must face the realities of where we are and reach out for the courage to move beyond our present place to a new place that may be possible.

Courage is the critical factor. It will always be easier to wallow in self-doubt and to find ourselves trapped by other people's expectations. Can we imagine the distractions that Jesus faced as he rode into Jerusalem? All the rejoicing and adulation. Our temptation is always to give up our own special purpose, to lay aside our own character and to become what others want us to be. Jesus faced these prospects of laying aside his destiny. After all, he could become king. He could be their hero and satisfy their longing for a political leader who would champion their cause.

Our temptations are less grandiose but no less distracting. There is not one of us who is not torn to be many people, inclined at times to turn aside from what is right and to do what is easy. In our personal lives, our new beginnings must always be wrestled out of our struggle with what is right and what is easy. We live most of our lives on this very road outside Jerusalem. It is a road between praise and conflict. That is where we live and where we must hammer out the meaning of our being here.

As a church, we will become disillusioned with the Christian faith if we misunderstand the meaning of new beginnings. It was precisely disillusionment that caused the disciples to turn away, to jump overboard, and to say "Count me out." The new beginning for dishonest Peter was not to be one without chaos or hurt or even death. Rather, the new day was a new way of understanding his own life. It was a new way of seeing his relationship within a small company of committed persons. God reshapes our expectations of ourselves. Again, the temptation is for us to scatter as a church every time there is a disagreement or turmoil. When the uncertainty escalates, we turn loose. Our destiny as a church must be shaped together. We are not a collection of discrete individuals. We are a colony of persons who are bound to each other in our joy and in our grief, in our doubt and in our faith, in our fear and in our hope.

The call of Jesus to his church is not a call to a clean slate. His call is not the naïve notion that everything is going to be alright. Instead, it is a call to begin to see ourselves as his people, in this place.

The church begins in Jerusalem. The church begins in the midst of the trouble and the turmoil. If our church triumphs as the people of God, it will be because we remain open to "God's new beginning." We cannot wait until everything is in order and we are all together in harmony and agreement. We must be willing to begin where we are, with our differences and our difficulties, with our anxiety and uncertainty. We must begin here in the Jerusalem in which God has placed us and become the church together.

But our human journey is marked not only by where we begin, but by where we are going. One of my favorite admonitions is that "If you don't know where you are going, you will probably end up somewhere else." The Scripture often speaks of Jesus "moving steadfastly." Our journey is always largely defined by where we are going. The fact is that we will get somewhere whether we are going anywhere or not. The issue is whether our lives are marked by purpose, by direction, or whether we bob adrift, becoming victims of time and culture. The crowds will always be there to tell us what we ought to do.

Despite all of the press of the crowds, Jesus was headed towards Jerusalem.

We have to know where we are going. We should understand that Jesus was not going for the purpose of dying. We have confused our faith. Jesus did not want to die. Jesus died because we killed him. He was murdered. He was innocently hanged.

Jesus' death was not some cosmic drama by which Jesus was trying to appease God's wrath. Jesus did not have to die for God's grace to be released upon a torn and crippled world. Jesus died because people, real ordinary people, were so threatened, so scared, so unable to cope with his life and actions, that they had to get rid of him. They had to try to destroy him. That is what happens when folks get scared. Fear will always twist and distort the world around us.

Where was Jesus going?

Jesus was not going to die. He was going to Jerusalem to do what he had done in Galilee, to live out the Father's will— to live it out, regardless of what might be the consequence of living out God's will.

Jesus' death was the result of that steadfastness, that purposeful journey in which he became the victim of hostility and anger, and in that conflict Jesus would choose even to die rather than to repudiate his commitment to love even his enemies without condition. He would accept even death rather than deny the ultimate reality of love and forgiveness. By the way he lived his life, he was saying that forgiveness—not death, not anger—is ultimately real! That is where he was going, to make that one truth clear.

We have gloried in the cross for so long that we have somehow forgotten how ugly it really was. The cross was cruel and grotesque. Jesus was compelled to live out the reality of love and grace, even in the midst of the torment and pain of people's fear and ugliness.

Our human journey is marked by where we are going. Our destination operates in every step we take. The human scene is filled with people who are living from event to event and whose journey will one day end without purpose or meaning.

On our human journeys, it is not only important where we begin and where we are going. It is important to know who is going with us. We should beware of the "Hallelujahs!" lest we begin to listen out for them.

On more than one occasion, the throngs pressed in upon Jesus, waiting for a word, waiting to be led, waiting to storm the gates of the city. They wanted to proclaim him king in the hope that a "king" would make all things right. After all, that is what a king is for—to establish right and to cast out the evil princes.

But Jesus chose a different kingdom. The crowds cheer but they disappear after the parade, leaving the streets littered with palm leaves and wasted placards. They do not come to go with him but to watch and to shout, to make noise. Many people may be present but few want to make the trip when darkness comes.

The church can sometimes behave mostly like the Palm Sunday crowd shouting their hosannas. But at its heart, the church is a quieter place. It is a place where we admit that we cannot make it alone and we reach out to take hold of one another. It is the place where grace and forgiveness take human shape in our everyday lives. Frankly, we don't live there very much. We mostly live scattered lives, driven by the wind, responding to one voice and then to another. But the church offers a still place where we find again our bearings and know who is with us. It is a place to get out of the crowd and be quiet.

The church itself, of course, has an uneven life. It is sometimes only one more frail human organization. But in those moments when the spirit of Jesus intrudes into our living, the church occurs. The church is something that happens. And when the church happens, Jesus comes alive here.

Who is going with you? That is the question that had to ring in Jesus' mind as he walked into Jerusalem. Our own lives will be indelibly marked by those who walk beside us— even in the tragedy and the quiet.

Our human journeys are very personal. There is an intimacy about our lives that can never be escaped. The triumphal entry on this day of Christian celebration reminds us that we must walk to the cadence of our own call. We cannot march to someone else's lead. We must find our call in the traffic of our own experience. The Christian family is composed of ordinary people, making their own journey, calling out hope and encouragement to one another.

As we celebrate the entrance to Holy Week, we realize that only a week away we will be celebrating, in all of its beauty and splendor, the joy and the triumph of the resurrection. My message is that it is a long way from Palm Sunday to Easter. It is a long way from the call to do God's will, with all the distractions of the crowds that want us to do and to be about other business. It is a long way to lay claim to the courage to be the church.

But there are no shortcuts. The road from Palm Sunday to Easter Sunday passes right through the darkness of Good Friday. Unless we are willing to hold on to one another in the darkness, we cannot rejoice with one another in the light.

Unless we are willing to walk through the turmoil and the terror of death, the agony and the injury of suffering, we cannot find the hope of Easter Sunday.

The road from Palm Sunday to Easter is a long journey. We cannot get there without beginning here. We must keep our eyes set on our ultimate call, and you and I, as the people of God, must learn to walk together.

Amen.

What Color Is a Month?

In search of answers, we analyze, dissect, experiment, examine, and offer hypotheses. But there is a peculiar thing about answers. Answers are rarely the end of the story. More often than not, an answer becomes a platform for posing new questions.

It is so because people are the kind of creatures that ask questions. Children are really best at it. In their innocence, children often ask difficult, uncomfortable, and even profound questions. Our inclination is to put their questions aside. But they persist. Questions such as "What is time?" "Will I die?" "Where did I come from?" Frankly, we have tried to teach children to ask better questions. "What is a touchdown?" "May I have a new play station?"

Even so, this distinctively human ability to step back, to interpret what we are doing and to ask questions sets us apart from the rest of the world. At times, the uncertainty that resides in our questions can be haunting. We, at times, long to be rid of them. Just play the music. Let's dance. Be done with the doubts and the mind-bending questions. We prefer to know all the answers, even to pretend, than to be plagued by the relentless questions.

My word of devotion is that the uncertainty and the "unsettledness" that takes hold of us can become the growing edge of our lives. And I add this word as well. The quality of our lives is determined, first of all, not by the kind of answers we propose but by the kind of questions we ask. If we put the wrong questions to life, we are likely to come out with the wrong answers.

When it comes to asking the right questions, the church is probably not helping very much. In the church, it often seems that we are trying to insulate ourselves from the troubling questions. We prefer to have the answers to life bound and reproduced in five easy doctrines.

But when we look closer, we are likely to discover that what the church has to offer for you and me is not an easy set of answers. Worship is a way of reaching out and holding on to each other. It is a way of calling out hope and encouragement to one another when the way is not clear and our future is clouded.

People who have all the answers do not need to find their way to worship. Only those of us who are troubled and for whom the way is not altogether clear, those of us for whom relationships often become fractured and confused need to stumble our way toward worship.

We do not come together in worship to listen to a formula for success or to chant a recipe for happiness. We come to worship simply because we need some help with our living. If we are to worship at all, we must worship as we are—with all of our questions and dilemmas. Worship can be our first step toward finding hope.

For all that we have gained from a worship experience that centers around the pulpit, we should also be sure of its liabilities. Listening to a sermon may be a passive experience, but worship never is. Worship engages us. Worship, when it occurs, helps us regain our bearings. Worship reminds us that life is more than the trivia that consumes our waking hours. Life is more than running to class, winning friends, and party time. Or, in the words of Jesus, life is more than food or clothing or drink. "Ask not what you shall drink or what you shall put on," Jesus says.

The words of Jesus surely do not suggest that food and clothing and shelter are not important matters. They are extremely vital issues especially if you live in Zimbabwe or Sri Lanka, or "under the bridge" in any large city.

Food will indeed relieve hunger. Clothing will shield us from the cold. Drink will quench our thirst. But we who are indeed well fed and well clothed make the point to which Jesus referred. Even in our good clothes, we are restless. Even with our full stomachs, we are not satisfied. We find ourselves chasing a new pleasure in the hope of finding joy.

In the midst of our restless pursuit, worship calls us to face a new set of questions. It causes us to face up to the dread of not knowing what to do, the dread of being dressed in style with nowhere to go. The frantic rites and the noise of our frequent celebrations will not take away the uneasiness that creeps in during the deep night when no one is watching.

So, worship may be, in part, about getting our questions right.

We should probably have a warning label on our letters of admissions to the university. And it should tell us that all of the knowledge we acquire will not be enough to make us feel good. Learning genuinely helps. It will make us more competent. It will help us succeed in a career. It will help us mature our relationships. It will help us gain food and clothing and drink.

But we need to learn this truth: Knowledge alone will not be enough. Knowledge alone will not bring solace to the soul or wisdom to the mind. In all of our learning, we must find a way of facing squarely into life's most compelling questions. Questions such as who is God or if there is a God, what is God like. We live everyday with other people. The Psalmist questions, "What is man?" Or—a less sexist translation— "What does it mean to be a person?" Or, we may ask, "Who am I?" "What on earth am I doing here?" These kinds of questions are larger than words. We answer them more with our choices and our relationships than with our speaking.

Look at the question of God. What is the name of your god? God's name can change, you know. That's called conversion. You can tell God's name by the acts you perform, by the attitudes you exhibit, by the words you speak. You can tell God's name by the swing of your step and by the path you make and the debris you leave behind you.

What is your god? God is that which is most important, most real in your life. God is that which concerns you ultimately, that which you value supremely. God may be a career. God may be a person. God may be a bank roll or an athletic achievement. God is anything to which you bow down. Some folks change gods frequently. They are like Eric Hoffer's "true believers," always in search of a cause, always looking for a new banner and always ready to join a new parade.

Some of us need to meet the question of who is God with more candid honesty. We need to force ourselves to examine how we're really answering this question. What really is the operating clue to our lives, not who do we say God to be but who do we live God to be.

The Christian faith offers us a clue to what God is like. The whole point of the Christian revelation is that in Jesus Christ we see what God is like, again not so much by the words Jesus speaks, but by the way Jesus engages life. It is a lot easier to believe in Jesus than to follow Jesus.

From Jesus we begin to learn that the meaning of life simply cannot be caught in words. That's why Jesus came. In Him, we see God's kind of life, we see God's kind of spirit. We see God's way of meeting people. We see God's kind of love. We see a kind of person who loves and forgives and who meets other people, not because they are lovable or forgivable or even fun to be with, but because loving and forgiving is the real heart of living.

So, what is the shape of your God? What is God's name? You can always tell God's name by the passion of your life.

Worship is also a good place to face into the issue of wondering about one another. We live in a world where loneliness causes us to be arrogant and where fear causes us to hurt each other. There is no guarantee that people as we know them are here to stay. We may slither off into nothingness and leave only a few stacked stones called Atlanta or Tokyo or New York to give any indication that anything unusual ever took place in this little corner of the galactic systems called Earth.

All of life is lived in relation to other people. How often are we alone? Most every waking hour reflects how we are answering this question. It is inescapable. Some of us may live as if the other person doesn't exist. We may ignore him. We may even pretend that she is not there. But we are fooling ourselves because she does exist and if we are honest we cannot live without her. All of us, whether we know each other or not, live in a common world. This is as good a day as any to face the truth that we cannot forever go it alone.

Who are these other people to you? What are people to you? The question is becoming more acute every day. Look at what is happening to us. We take our shuttles into space. But the end of the search is not the moon or Mars or Jupiter or the rings of Saturn. The end of the search is ourselves. We want to know who we are. Here on earth we're just as frantic. Exploring the control of genetic defects and the control of inherited characteristics and the control of death itself.

Information, just the facts, we can get from science but our sense of the meaning of life we must gain from our own choices. All of the information in the world will not make us feel good or dispel our uneasiness. The Christian faith simply offers us one direction, one way of seeing our life with one another. It reminds us that we were created to love and that only as we learn to love will we learn to live.

But I worry. I worry because Christian love becomes so easily confused with superficial and sentimental niceness. But Jesus does not speak to our sentiments. In his commandment to love one another, Jesus is not asking us to resolve to like everybody. He is speaking rather to our wills. What do we will for people? He is asking us to act for the good of others whether we like them or not.

Lucy's little brother Linus screamed at Charlie Brown: "I love humanity—it's *people* I can't stand!"

Finally, I believe our worship together can bring us to the question of "Who am I?" In a sense, this is the most personal of all human questions. Not only can no one answer it for you, no one can even ask it for you. Life is a process of discovering who we are. Each of us is a unique, irreplaceable individual with certain distinctive gifts and we live under a divine responsibility to become who we were created to be. Perhaps the greatest task of our life is to unlock the power of our souls. The philosopher Socrates knew that when he said, "Know thyself," and his student Plato added, "The unexamined life is not worth living." With Dan Leno we should ask, "Ah! What is man? Wherefore does he why? Whence did he whence? Whither is he withering?"

The answering of such questions involves a lifetime. For life is a journey. Who are you? Are you a Xerox copy, a mere photographic reproduction, an ideological clone, or a person, genuine and real, striving to be who you are and not what others would make you to be.

I submit to you that these are the final questions that should not and cannot be put aside. And more importantly, they really are the religious questions of life. The basic religious questions are not shall I go to Sunday school or even shall I go to church. Years ago, there was one of those TV "doctor programs" entitled, "Ben Casey." The beginning of that program was near to the heart of the matter when it began with these words, "Man, woman, life, death, infinity." These are the basic religious problems: Who is God? What do I do with other people? Who am I? These are the religious questions.

You and I live in a tangled world for which we bear the burden of untangling. If we are to do so, we need a different kind of evangelism. Instead of proclaiming a remote distant gospel, we need to care about people up close. It will simply not be enough to paint "Jesus Saves' on all the rocks in public parks. Caring will mean helping people come to grips with their own meaning.

Easy answers are easy mostly because they are unrelated to the tough questions. My point is concluded by a verse composed by a friend named Bruce Evans.

> *How hot is an inch?* Asked he,
>   Answer me simply and quick.
> I don't go for mumbling around
>   Words just make me sick.

> *What is time?* pleaded she,
>   Answer me yes or no.
> Someone else has been asking me
>   And I simply have to know.

> *When is orange?* queried another.
>   And don't tangle me up with words.

All this complicated stuff
    Is something for the birds.

What color is a month? asked he,
    Please answer me black or white.
Cause I'm headed now for a heavy date
    And I don't wanta be thinkin' tonight.
        On and on
        Drone and drone
Answer me quickly,
    I must know;
Black or white,
    Yes or no?

Dear God, my prayer will be this night
    Not for answers nice and light
But give us wisdom by thy might
    to somehow get our answers right.

Amen.

Principles, Priorities, and Promises

Being religious is not a Sunday morning affair. The Christian faith, if it matters at all, must engage us as we go to work and worry about children. The Christian faith is present amidst conflicts between children and parents, in overcoming hurt feelings, and in the times when we are afraid. That is where we live and those are the streets where we meet God, if we are to meet God at all.

Ordinary life and belief converge on the playing field of hammering out the principles and the priorities and promises that guide us.

Most of us like to think of ourselves as people of principle. The problem for most of us is not that we have too few principles. The problem is more likely that we have too many.

We become weighted down by a barrel full of principles; principles piled on top of principles. As a result, we do not take any of them very seriously. People want us to be so many things. The expectations of spouses and employers, of teachers and friends, crowd in upon us. We long to satisfy everyone's idea of what we ought to be and how we ought to behave.

We discover early in our lives that people will stand in line to tell us how to dress and how to vote. They will tell us the friends we ought to make, and the careers we ought to pursue. Some people want to push us a little to the left and others will nudge us a little to the right. Everybody has a set of principles for us.

Jesus came into a world that was weighted down by tomes of religious principles. The Jewish religion had added interpretation on top of interpretation, rules on top of rules. The result was a depressing load of religious expectation and baggage. The world of being a good Jew had become so complicated that only the professionally religious could keep up. For ordinary people like you and me, the world of religion had, frankly, grown into something largely irrelevant, more a burden to carry than light by which to find our way.

So, my first word for you is this: Live by fewer principles. I believe that to be Jesus' point when he was questioned by a learned man—a lawyer.

The lawyer said to Jesus, "What shall I do to inherit eternal life?" What ought I do to experience life that has no boundaries?

Jesus said, "You tell me. . . . Amidst all the complex volumes of religious principles and admonitions, what is the first principle?"

And he answered, "Love God with all your heart and all your soul, with all your strength and all your mind, and love your neighbor as youself."

And Jesus said quietly, "Do this and you will live."

Jesus didn't say, do this *and* come to church and you will live. It was not, do this *and* read your Bible and you will live. It was not, do this *and* pray always and you will live. All of these may be worthy. But, first things first. Love God with all your heart and all your soul and all your strength and all your mind and take care of each other, and you will live. First things first.

Live by fewer principles. Here is a principle you can live by. This principle will, without question, change the story of your life—nothing less. This one principle will change the steps you take. It will change the work you do, the families you raise, and the person you become.

The principle is this: All real, ordinary living is relating, and relating at its highest is loving. Love God with all your heart and soul and strength and mind and take care of one another. Do this and you will live.

No verses to memorize, no creeds to recite, no volumes of doctrine to master. The first and most important word for living our everyday lives is this: As we learn to love, we will learn to live.

Loving without condition, loving without any prerequisites, loving without any "ifs' is the one gift that will set you free. Love with abandon. Love unconditionally. When we find the courage to love, we become free of fear. Loving is the one gift, the only gift, that will set you free.

But, we do not live by principle alone. Regardless of what we believe in, our everyday lives are also driven by priorities, that is, how we put our principles to work. Love that does not make you act differently is nothing more than dead language. Love changes every connection in your life.

For most of us, the only way to determine our priorities is by the looking glass. We look back to see where we have been. Our tracks reveal our priorities.

So, the truth is that we do not have to choose our priorities. They will choose us. While we do not have the option of living without priorities, we do have the option of being blind to our priorities.

After all, you and I live lives that are very full. We have lots of things to do. We have places to go, appointments to keep. We have projects to finish and letters to write. We have e-mails to read and parties to attend. We have dancing to do.

Our lives are often like overstuffed suitcases—bursting at the seams. We are occupied and preoccupied. Have you ever thought about what it means to be preoccupied? Being preoccupied means being busy before you get there. We worry about things before they happen. We worry about whether we will get a promotion. We worry about whether our children will succeed, whether we can balance books this month. We worry about whether we are good enough. We worry about diseases we might get. We worry about whether our parents will stay together.

Jesus looks at our worry-filled lives through a different lens. Jesus does not respond to our worries by trying to pull us away from the events and activities and people who make up our daily calendars. Jesus does not tell us that all our engagements are unimportant or useless. Far from it.

Rather, Jesus sets out to change our center of gravity. Think about it. Your center of gravity is the center of what finally matters to you. Jesus wants us to relocate, to reposition, our center of self-understanding, to reposition what matters to us.

In the course of our careers and families, you and I are required to do many things. We take on many causes, go many places, accept many jobs. The issue is whether there is any order to what we do, or do we just do whatever comes next? Is there a center of gravity that gives us some sense of balance? All causes are not created equal.

It is important to understand that the Christian faith does not call upon us—nor does Jesus—to set aside our complex and busy lives. Our lives are complex. Relationships are complex and difficult. The truth is that you and I need some kind of center point that can help us figure out what is really important.

Searching for priorities, Jesus frankly uses words we wouldn't use. He said, "Seek first the Kingdom." You and I are not much into kings and kingdoms. We don't much cotton to hierarchies and monarchies. But, let's see if we can bring these words down to earth.

Taking hold of the Kingdom means seeing the world, seeing yourself, seeing other people, from God's point of view. Startling! Try seeing your husband from God's point of view, especially when you are annoyed with him. Try seeing your child from God's point of view, especially when she has misbehaved. The Kingdom of God is not a different world out yonder somewhere. The Kingdom of God is in our town. "Seek first the Kingdom" means looking at your sister, looking at your son, looking at your boss from a different point of view.

Setting our hearts on the Kingdom means shifting the center of gravity.

When Jesus speaks of shifting our priorities, he sets it over against the concern for food and clothing and shelter. There is no hint that these matters are unimportant. Ask someone who is hungry whether food is important. Ask the homeless whether shelter is significant. Food and clothing and shelter are cited precisely because they are universally important.

We often classify people by their patterns of acquisition and consumption—the clothes they wear, the cars they drive, the places they live. The Fortune 500 lists people by how much they have acquired. Most mass advertising on TV is aimed at managing and controlling what people consume.

Jesus never suggests that either acquisition or consumption is evil. Rather, Jesus speaks to the priorities that govern our lives. If we define our lives first and chiefly by acquisition and consumption, we will finally lose out. End of story. It all comes to nothing. Our consuming will end. Our acquisition will run out. Our barns will decay. Our stocks will be sold.

Our bank accounts will be closed. Our clocks will stop. End of story.

Jesus wants to refocus us on priorities that are not nearly so fragile. Jesus wants to help us find a measure for our lives that is not so fleeting as the calendar. Surely, most of us want to add one more day, one more year, one more decade, to our lives. That is good, but we should not get confused. Adding days does not add life. It only delays death. Days are too fragile a commodity to measure our lives by.

Seeing our ordinary lives from God's point of view changes how life looks and feels. Following Jesus radically shifts the priorities that govern us. We are called upon to measure our lives, not by what we have gained but by what we have given. A radical change. The measure of our lives shifts from how much we have acquired to how deeply we have loved. Not where do you live but whom do you care about?

The principle is: Love God with all your heart and soul and strength and mind and take care of one another. The new center of gravity is not how much have we gained, how much have we acquired or consumed, but how much have we given, how deeply have we loved. The Christian faith simply changes, radically changes, what it means to be here.

One final word. I believe that the principles we live by and the priorities that govern us are sustained only by the power of promise.

Every one of us is on a journey toward the promised land. Take away our journey toward the promised land and there can be no escape from the bondage of Egypt or the bondage of consumption and acquisition.

In our daily lives, you and I are pulled along by our yearning for some promised land. Ask yourself: What is the promised land for which you are yearning? It may be a job paying six figures. It may be a brick house with a three-car garage. It may be an All-American family with 2.5 children.

Promises, promises. Our principles and priorities are sustained solely by the ultimate power of God's promise. The promise of God—listen to it, etch it into your soul: Grace will prevail. Love will endure. God is with us without condition.

Tuck this truth away. The hope for your future does not ultimately rest upon whether you get your principles right or your priorities in order. Our ultimate hope rests in the promise that God will stay with us even when we fail our principles and even when we lose sight of our priorities. God is not with us just when we do right. The promise is that God is with us even when we mess up.

Our personal journeys will not be finally defined by whether we win or lose. The truth is that we will both win and lose. Our winning will sometimes be our greatest defeats. And some of our losses will be our highest triumphs. The promise of life is not whether we will win or lose. Succeed or fail. We will succeed and we will be defeated.

The journey to every person's promised land always goes through the wilderness. We get bruised and baked by the searing heat. There is no other way to the promised land. There is no path to the promised land that is free of trouble and turmoil. We are people who ache. We are people who impose pain on one another in hopes that it will make us feel better. It never does.

We sometimes get disillusioned, wondering if there is even a place called the promised land. But listen to this word: The promised land is not a land to be found. It is a promise to claim. The promised land is not about land; it is about a promise.

So, hear and claim this ultimate promise: God is with us no matter what. God is not with us only if we believe the right beliefs, belong to the right church, or do the right thing. The promise of grace is that God is with us—no matter what.

So, pack your principles and priorities. They will help you chart your journey. But, they will not alone keep hope alive. What will keep hope alive is believing deep down that God is with us.

Listen to the promise: I will deliver you from the land of trouble and hurt, and bring you out on eagle's wings unto myself so that you—you and I, here and now, may be a community of priests, looking out for each other, so that you and I can live for a different, more enduring purpose. You, God says, you are and will remain, a special treasure.

That is God's promise. Go from this sanctuary and taste the freedom of unfettered grace.

Amen.

Holy Ground

Every person's life turns out to be a story and because our stories are as different as the stars, each of our lives occupies a very special place in the world. The contours of your life are different from those of any other and we together make up a spectrum called the people of God. We are God's light for the world.

The stories of our lives—yours and mine—do not seem extraordinary. But think about it for a moment and you are likely to recall certain events that turned out to shape and color the rest of your life.

From Holy Scripture, we listen to a brief story that shaped the rest of the life of a man named Moses. It was on a spot that came to be called "holy ground" that Moses took his first step toward the Promised Land. And as you listen to Moses' story, think about your own personal story. Think about the unexpected bushes that have flamed up in your own life and made you a different person. Some encounter. Some event. Some individual. Some relationship that put fire into your soul.

Now Moses kept the flock of Jethro, his father-in-law, the priest of Midian; and he led the flock to the backside of the desert, and came to the mountain of God, even to Horeb.

And the angel of the Lord appeared unto him in a flame of fire out of the midst of a bush; and he looked, and, behold, the bush burned with fire and the bush was not consumed.

And Moses said, I will now turn aside, and see this great sight, why the bush is not burnt.

And when the Lord saw that he turned aside to see, God called unto him out of the midst of the bush, and said, Moses, Moses. And he said, Here am I.

And He said, Draw not nigh hither; put off thy shoes from off thy feet, for the place where you are standing is holy ground.   (Exodus 3:1-5)

Every day, we find Moses pretty much where we find ourselves—wandering about in the wilderness of his work. Moses was tending a small herd of sheep. They were not even his own sheep. So it is with us. We mostly tend other people's sheep, handle other people's money, keep other people's books, teach other people's children, look at other people's X-rays, and analyze other people's problems.

Like much of our work, Moses' work was also really tough. Wandering on the back slopes, trying to escape the sun, looking for a few green sprouts peeking through the craggy terrain. You can see his sheep stripping dry leaves from dwarfed trees and chewing on scraggly bushes. It was hot. No oak trees. No lush green meadows. Just dust and rocks. It was desert. Dry. For Moses, the brutal desert sun was a long way from the palaces of Egypt where he had once lived.

But it was here, in this remote and desolate place, not in the plush palaces of Egypt, that Moses saw something he had never seen before. We ought to tuck this truth away. It sometimes takes a barren, deserted place to be able to see. Moses was startled by a blazing bush. Sweating from the summer heat, he walked a little closer in order to get a better look.

As Moses gets closer, you and I overhear the most dramatic part of this story. Moses heard a voice. And the voice said, "Take off your shoes, Moses. You are standing on holy ground."

You have to be kidding. Here Moses is in the desert sun, doing his job, longing for relief from the heat. Here in this sun-parched, God-forsaken territory Moses hears the absurd sounding word that he is standing on "holy ground."

Think about it. We would somehow expect holy ground to be more appealing—perhaps a trout stream or an awesome mountain gaping into clouds or perhaps a cathedral with stained-glass windows. Instead, Moses is told that here on this barren deserted back slope of Mount Horeb, he is standing on holy ground.

The desert is tough terrain. Nobody lived there. Nobody could survive there for long. Even to eke out a daily living, Moses had to wander from slope to slope in search of food and shade. Hardly a place that you or I or Moses would consider calling holy.

So I wonder: What does it take to make a place holy? My hunch is that where you and I live is more akin to the back slope than it is to the palaces of Egypt.

The plain truth is that we expect hallowed places to be more serene—different from where we tend our sheep and open our mail. After all, our everyday places—well, they are so plain and everyday. They are good places. But they are rather ordinary. They have their porches and swings. They have their broken shutters and rusted pipes. Our towns are ordinary. They have an Exxon gas station on one corner, with another corner anchored by Burger King. The banks are brick. They look a bit like vaults. The grocery stores have a special on two heads of lettuce. They have a café where you can get a meat and two vegetables for $6.99 and a post office with posters of the most wanted. They have a mall with a big open corridor for flea-market sales and for taking pictures of Santa at Christmas. The streets are dotted with office buildings that have plate-glass windows and monotone furnishings. It is, after all, our town—a good town, plain, expected, but ordinary.

Today may be as good a day as any, and better than most, to be startled into hearing God's truth. The truth is this: The extraordinary often gets hidden beneath the rugged terrain of the ordinary.

It is easy enough for us to hear that Jerusalem is a holy place, that Mecca is a holy place, that the Vatican is a holy place. It is more difficult, more disturbing, even more surprising for us to hear that *our place* is a holy place.

That's God's word for us today. Look for holiness here. God is going to come to us where we are. Listen out for God—in the midst of your common routine. Look for God in the twists and turns of your own familiar path. We must learn to see God through the dust of our own difficulties.

You and I are mostly like Moses—preoccupied with our own choices, our own anxieties, worrying about our children, preoccupied with hostile feelings and broken promises. We cannot hear God. We are barely managing to keep our sheep. The extraordinary gets consumed, eaten up, by the ordinary. We are simply too busy to let the divine intrude into our lives.

But understand this: the extraordinary is not ordinary. When God takes hold of our soul, it changes what we do and how we act. It changes how we relate and it inevitably changes where we go from here. Taking seriously God's presence will take us from the wilderness to the promised land.

So, come along and let's probe the terrain of where we may find God and listen to the lessons of Moses.

Lesson one: We find God in ordinary places.

Quite simply, I find God on the quadrangle at Mercer. You find God at the teller's window or in the produce section at Kroger. You find God in the kitchen or in the boardroom, in the classroom or in the courthouse. We find God where we actually live. We find God while we tend our sheep and write our letters, and compose our lyrics. We find God where we actually live our everyday lives. And, like Moses, we are always startled to meet God there.

The crisp, enduring lesson is this. The burning bushes are not out there in somebody else's wilderness. God comes to us in your wilderness and in mine.

The place to find God is where we find ourselves living out our lives. If you and I are to find this extraordinary God of grace and forgiveness, we will have to meet God, be startled by God's presence in ordinary, everyday places.

Moses can teach us a second lesson: The God of the extraordinary is to be found among ordinary people.

God does not come to us most often by way of high priests or prophets, or even preachers. God mostly comes to us in the hands and the faces of one another. God comes to us in the intimate and powerful relationships that color the stories of our lives. The most basic work of God lies in changing how we meet each other. The lessons of faith are not about going to church or how to get to heaven. The most important lessons of faith are about changing how we live with each other.

And God knows that is where we need the most help. Our lives together become fractured and frayed. We meet in the corridors and the storefront, in the theatre, and in the bedroom. We bump into each other in so many places, yet we are frightened to really meet each other. The blazing light of

God's presence turns the places where we meet each other into holy ground. It was only the light of a burning bush that could show Moses how he could face a pharaoh who loathed him and family and friends who distrusted him.

To be honest, our life together becomes tangled and tired. We suffer hurt feelings. We speak angry words. It's called the desert.

That's because life with each other is tough terrain. Our noisy world is a mixture of crying and laughing, of hope and apprehension, of chatter and silence. We are sometimes quiet when we are full of things we want to say, and we sometimes talk nonstop when we have nothing to say.

Why is it? Because that's our kind of wilderness.

And it is precisely in this kind of world that we can meet the startling presence of God. If we cannot find the reflections of God in the faces of each other, we are unlikely to meet God at all. But we need to hear this word. We underestimate the power of God's presence. It will be a transforming, life-changing event to run into God in the desert of hatred and malice and distrust. Like a blaze that will not go out, God will change the way we live with each other.

So, God calls us to this extraordinary possibility of building different relationships out of those that have become broken and battered and abandoned. If you want to see God, look for God not simply in preachers. Look for God in the eyes of your teacher or the postman, or the checkout clerk, or in the eyes of your friend, or even your enemy. Look for God in those you like and in those you dislike, because those people are God's greatest gift to you.

Let's come along. Let's listen out for a final lesson from our teacher, Moses.

The lesson is this: Holy ground is to be found in our own kind of earth—an earth that is scorched with trouble, an earth that is haunted by dreadful disease.

You and I, try as hard as we may, cannot find a land that is free of turmoil. We cannot walk on ground that is undisturbed by hurt.

However much we would like it, holy ground is not a safe haven from the brutal desert sun. Life is not like that. In real life, we get wounded. Our lips crack. Our skin wrinkles. Our hair grays. Holy ground has to be trodden out of the rugged terrain that causes bruises and blisters.

Holy ground calls upon us not to define our lives by the bruises. Do not define your life by the blisters or the brokenness. Moses was utterly brokenhearted by the rejection of his family and his friends in Egypt. At Mt. Horeb, he was broken down not only by the heat of the sun but by the lonely isolation—away from everybody he loved. We too limp along because of hurt feelings and angry words, because of fear and dread.

Life with God is lived on a road that yields difficulty and trouble. You and I know firsthand the searing heat of a life that has been wrecked by disappointment. The fact is that the world is a troublesome place. We live in the kind of world where people are prone to be hateful to each other, where diseases invade, and where people's physical lives deteriorate.

For goodness sake, the message of Moses is not that trouble isn't painful. Moses' message certainly is not that despair doesn't disrupt what we are doing. Moses knew what it meant to ache, but hear the message of Moses: *The desert is not the end of the journey. Life is more than the scorching sun and the desert rocks.* Moses learned that lesson by the light of a burning bush.

If we are to know God, we cannot wait for better pastures. We have to look up from our labors and see the reality of God ablaze in our ordinary places. Look up and see the presence of God in the faces of ordinary people and within the ordinary events that are shaping the story of our lives.

If we want to know God, we have to be ready to see our places as holy ground. Here is the gospel of holy ground. You are going to meet God when you put your arms around someone who is bent over with grief. You will find God in your words of encouragement and hope to someone who feels beaten down. You will see God in your willingness to listen to somebody who thinks that nobody understands.

You and I live in a world that is often under the siege of ill will and mindless criticism. That's the way people behave. We should make our own confessions. We often put one another down and even scoff at one another's mistakes. Today let us hear the gospel. The gospel is that you and I can move from the desert of despair and distrust to the promised land of hope and grace. Bit by bit. Step by step. We can begin to transform hatefulness. We can live beyond fear.

Scorched earth or holy ground. The difference turns out to be not in the ground, but how we walk on it. The earth can be dry and lifeless or it can be holy and fruitful. This is the prospect we face even today with our brother, Moses.

Scorched earth. You have lived there. It sounds like this: "I will forgive him if he straightens up and does right." Scorched earth. "He doesn't deserve to be forgiven." Scorched earth. "I will love her if she lives by my rules." Scorched earth. That's living in the desert.

Holy Ground. Loving people who don't deserve to be loved. Holy ground. Embracing people who don't measure up. Holy ground. Loving people, acting for the good of people you don't' like. Holy ground. Wrapping the wounds of people you don't know. That's living by the light of the burning bush.

God's call is for us to walk toward one another and toward our own future with a new fire. We, like Moses, are inclined to walk under our own power. We want to chart our own course, solve our own problems, cure our own ills. We tend our own sheep.

The gospel for Moses and the gospel for you and me is that when the fire of God blazes up in our souls, God will change, God will utterly change, the story of our lives.

Through the burning bush, God is calling us to a new kind of journey, a journey that gives us the courage to forgive and the willingness to look out for each other. The journey of faith is a long journey. We sometimes get lost and wander around. We break down and have to be picked up. It is a long journey. A journey that has twists and turns, steep hills and sharp curves; it has starts and stops.

But take heart. Listen to Moses. He knew about the starts and stops. Walk by the light of the fire of God. And that fire will transform our wilderness into a place we can call the Promised Land.

Amen.

Amazing Grace

Sunday has come and we climb the hill toward a place we call sanctuary. Sanctuary is a place to come in from the noise. Sanctuary is the place where we can be free of the pulling and tugging that wears us down, free of chasing after one more success.

Sunday has come. So, we huddle here in the shade of sanctuary, feeling a little bewildered. Day after day we are committed to so many causes—families to raise, profits to make, appointments to keep, calls to return. We are going in so many directions, wearing so many hats, putting on so many faces.

But, Sunday has come. Perhaps, we can rest here for a moment and be quiet. No loyalties to prove, no questions to answer, no reports to type, no bills to pay, no loads to lift. Because Sunday has come, and God says simply "Come and rest."

We do not make our way into sanctuary to pretend that life always feels good. It does not. We do not come to sanctuary, of all places, to put on the face of piety and make believe that everything is alright. The altar is the place, the one place, where we can take off our make-believe faces, confess our troubles, and abandon ourselves to the simplicity of grace. Amazing grace.

Sunday has come and I speak a simple word of grace. Grace is Sunday's most important gift. Remember this. Tack it to your doorstep. Sear it into your heart. Grace is God's first and last word. Amidst all the shifting sand and the bitter winds that sometimes knock us off our feet, grace is a place to stand. Grace is the only ground that will not shift beneath our feet.

You and I are people with relationships that become fractured and frayed. Our lives together cause bruises and bumps. We are ordinary people, living here or there, whose lives get tattered and whose relationships become crumpled and sometimes crippled. That's where you and I live.

Sunday has come to remind us that there is nothing more sacred, no journey quite so hallowed, as the journey toward recovering once again a center for our souls. We need a center, a defining center. We are pulled and yanked in so many directions. There are plenty of people who want to stand us here, to move us a little to the right or to nudge us a little toward the left. They become agitated and aggravated if we do not stay in our assigned places.

Grace is a radically new kind of place to stand. I am reminded of the thundering words of Martin Luther when he was jolted by the unencumbered power of grace. Luther was a man set free from the struggle to prove himself worthy to God. From this radical vision of grace he proclaimed, "Here I stand. I can do no other. God help me." Luther made trouble. Luther's life as a priest would have worked out fine if he had simply stood where he had been told to stand.

But, Martin Luther came in from the icy cold of a religion that had grown sterile and empty, into the sanctuary of grace. Meeting grace for the first time changed everything. Luther's problem, and Jesus' problem as well, was that they would not stay put. In the process of standing up, Luther stumbled over the entire Roman church.

Jesus stumbled over a religion that had come to trust and rely upon its own systems of belief. Sounds familiar. The Pharisees and the princes of Rome were not bad people. They were not into crucifying people for Friday night fun. They were afraid. Jesus would not stand where he had been told to stand. Jesus spoke the gospel in a new voice. And the good people of his time had to protect the church they loved.

We have a desperate need to put people in their places. We divide them by race and gender, by class and position. And then we are shocked when sexism and racism and religious intolerance begin to haunt us. The truth is, that racism and sexism and countless other prejudices are our way of keeping people in their place.

That's our kind of world. And let us understand that religion has become a part of that kind of world. Religion becomes more our creation than God's. Religion is one more way of sorting people into various camps—the saved and the unsaved, the holy and the unholy, the forgiven and the unforgiven, the good guys and the bad. Then, God becomes our excuse for intolerance and prejudice.

But, when the light of Sunday breaks through all our elaborate religious systems, we are left with grace and grace alone. Amazing grace. Cut through all the theories and the ritual. Grace is all that's left.

So, let us hear the Christian gospel in all of its radical simplicity. At least for a moment, set aside all the complex religious systems, the plethora of denominations. Grace is God's word, and in Jesus, we see what grace looks like up close. There is nothing magical about the Christian faith. No magic, no smoke and mirrors.

The Christian gospel is grace. Listen to its sound. Grace means that God is on our side. God is in us. God is with us. God is for us. No mountain which we climb, no valley into which we fall, will cause God to walk away. God is for us and God is going to stay with us to the end. That is the startling, blazing light from God.

That's Sunday's word for us today. It is grace upon grace. No limits, no conditions. The Christian gospel is not a religion to affirm or a church to join. The Christian gospel is Jesus.

In Jesus, God comes to our side. In our loneliness, says we are not alone; in our guilt, says we are forgiven; in our chains, says we are free; in our fear, says we are safe.

The word of faith, if we will listen to its wonder, is that you and I live in the arms of grace. Simple, unfettered, reckless caring is what grace looks like in ordinary life. Caring without regard for whether somebody deserves to be cared for. Grace means listening to somebody who thinks that nobody understands. It means wrapping the wounds of some person you don't even know. That's the power of grace.

That's God's way. God's love is not based on whether we are good enough, or if we know the right words to recite, or if we "do right." God's love is simple. It is unlimited and unconditional.

The truth of grace is so very difficult for us to believe. Frankly, we mostly do life in a different way. We like people who like us. We are good to people who are good to us. We care for people who deserve to be cared for. We give to people who give to us. None of this foolishness of taking care of people who hate your guts. Grace, after all, is a radical and ridiculous gospel.

But, Sunday has come. So, let the light stream in. Grace is God's word. It is grace upon grace. Grace changes the center of gravity for our lives.

We have been mistaken. We do not have to repent, or to confess. We don't have to do anything to win God's forgiveness. Forgiveness is God's word to us. That is what grace means. Grace is sometimes more light than we can stand.

Grace, amazing grace, changes how life looks and it changes how we look at life. When the light breaks, we begin to see people, friends and enemies, as children of God's grace. The startling, persistent news of the gospel is that God is not with us because we belong to the right religion, or even because we read our Bible. God is with us because that is who God is and that's what God is like.

So, listen again to the lessons of grace.

Lesson 1. Grace means that you matter. There is only one you. Every person matters. Grace doesn't mean that God's going to be with us if we do right. Grace means that God is by our side, no matter what.

Lesson 2. Grace means that we don't have to be afraid. We are hateful to one another, mostly because we are afraid of each other. When people are afraid of each other, they either flee or they fight, often with words, sometimes with guns. Neither the piercing attack of words nor the brutality of bullets will ever match the power of grace to overcome hatred and fear. Bullets will not do it. Hateful words will not do it. Bitterness will not do it. Only grace will set us free to love.

Lesson 3. Grace will give us the power to behave differently. On many interstates, the paved shoulders to the highways have grooves or ridges on them, so that when we drift away from the lane, we will hear a rumble as a warning. Rules, regulations, and laws are rather like the grooves. They help us find our way. The law will not make you a better person.

Last year, there was a television ad, either for Visa or MasterCard. It began by saying, "MasterCard will not make you a better person." But the ad concludes that it may actually make you a better person.

Take this truth away with you. Pack it in your bags and carry it with you for the rest of your life. It may be the only thing I say today that is genuinely important.

Grace, not Visa or MasterCard.

Grace, not rules, regulations, or Moses' law.

Grace, alone, will make you a better person.

Lesson 4. Grace means that we are not here to shout empty religious slogans and demean one another with trivial Christianity. Grace means we are here to be light to people who are trying to crawl out of the shadows. Grace means that we are not here to recite the right religious ideology. We are here to forgive. Grace means that we are not here to require that people embrace the latest form of Christian or Baptist orthodoxy. We are here to embody the gospel in reckless caring, to give people hope. Everyone of us is somebody's best hope. You are somebody's best hope. Grace means that we are here to help people in Jesus' name and to ask questions later.

So, grace is not something terribly grandiose. It is not a theological proposition. Grace is not even about keeping the church alive at all costs. Grace is a simpler word. Grace means to heal the sick. Grace means to help the poor. Grace means to shelter the homeless and to teach the ignorant. Grace means setting people free of disease and free of prejudice. Grace means looking out for people who are lonely, taking up for people who are powerless. Grace changes every priority.

Lesson 5. Finally, grace means, above all else, that God believes in us. I have learned that growing up and living is a series of victories and defeats. I have been defeated. If we are not careful, we can begin to define our lives by the defeats. If we do, we fall into a descending spiral of depression and despair, trying to climb out, trying to be somebody, trying our best to believe in God even when things are tough. The word of grace begins somewhere else. The real hope of grace is not that we believe in God. The real and enduring hope of grace is that God believes in us.

So, let us listen again for grace.

The lesson of grace is that God is not remote, hidden behind the walls of temples or synagogues. God is not tucked away in cathedrals and inner sanctums. God is with us here.

Meet God here. Meet God in the kitchen, at the dinner table. Meet God at the checkout counter at Walgreen's, across the teller's desk. Meet God in the halls of commerce. Meet God in the eyes of your friend, even in the face of your enemy.

Learn to live with grace. Anger and bitterness corrodes the human spirit and binds us into knots.

Grace and grace alone will set us free—free to hope and free to love.

On that gospel, I believe we can stake our lives. Sunday has come. So, come and rest in the arms of grace.

Amen.

Becoming the Truth

Several years ago, the movie *Liar, Liar* was winning the box office sweepstakes. More contortionist than actor, Jim Carrey played a lawyer who makes his living telling lies. We can hope that Carrey is a caricature of lawyers. Being in the business of educating lawyers, I have learned that it is not an uncommon perception that truth is rarely the first order of business for a lawyer. The overwhelming view is that their point is to win—the truth be damned.

Frankly, we get terribly confused about truth. No wonder we are confused. When the judge says, "Do you swear to tell the truth, the whole truth and nothing but the truth," she is wanting you to assure the court that what you say will correspond with what you actually know. Without that baseline precondition, the court is left to wallow in the muddle of empty rhetoric. On the other hand, if we ask whether someone is a true friend, we are using truth in a very different way. What we really mean is whether his friendship, his relationship is reliable and trustworthy. Will he be there in the morning?

In my former life, I regularly taught courses in logic. When I became an administrator, I learned that logic alone is rarely enough. Life, yours and mine, turns out to be a lot more than logic.

Logic's answer to what is truth is very different, radically different from life's answer to what is truth.

In logic, true and false are characteristics of propositions. In order to determine whether a statement is true or false, we look to see if what we say corresponds to what is actually happening. Someone says, "It is raining today." If you want to know whether that statement is true, you look out the window or go outside. If you go outside without an umbrella and it's raining you will get wet. But logic quickly reminds us that getting wet alone will not be enough to establish the truth of whether it's raining. Someone could be working on the roof and spill water on your head as you walk out. But soon by sight and touch, you can tell whether it is raining. Observation establishes the truth.

Some statements pose a far greater problem to tell if they are true by observation. For example, "Love endures." "God exists." "Murder is wrong." There are no observations you can make to determine whether those statements are true or false. Observation alone is not enough.

Logic has one other avenue for establishing truth. Since some things cannot be easily observed, we try to determine if they fit with what else we know to be true. The truth and falsehood of mathematics depends upon this kind of coherence. 2+2=4 is true because it fits with what else we know to be true. We don't know that simply by observation. 2 apples + 2 apples equals 4 apples. Observation. But what about 2 raindrops plus 2 raindrops? Looks like one big raindrop. Their "fourness" is not nearly so evident.

Coherence or Observation. My point is that logic has its ways of determining truth.

Some folk have great difficulty dealing with religion or with faith because they cannot make faith fit into the canons of logic. They say, unless I can observe it or deduce it, I will not believe it.

The point of our faith is that life is more than logic and truth is more than propositions. The most important and enduring lessons of life will not turn out to be lessons of logic. They are lessons about relating—relating to yourself, relating to other people, relating to what the world is all about. I believe that one of life's most basic lessons is the discovery that life is more than logic.

We are enamored in our western culture with the power of facts. We are even consumed by the facts of our faith. The facts turn out to be trivial. Was the Virgin Birth of Jesus a fact? It is a trivial question.

When Jesus said "The truth shall set you free," he did not say the facts will set you free. The goal of religion is not to get all our facts in order—a neat set of propositions we can believe to be true without a doubt. Faith is filled with doubt. Ask Peter about doubt. Faith can never be reduced to facts. The Christian faith is not about agreeing to anybody's set of facts. The facts of faith will not make us whole. The fact of Jesus, the fact of his death, the fact of his resurrection will not bring us life. Faith is not about facts.

The Christian faith is about coming face to face with a whole new order of truth. The truth of the Christian faith is not a statement to accept or a fact to affirm. The truth of which Jesus speaks, the truth that will set us free, is a way of life to embrace. Jesus did not say to his disciples, "Learn my teachings and you will be my disciples." Jesus did not say, "Go away and learn to recite my words and you will be my disciples." He said something far more simple and direct and life changing. Jesus said, "Come and follow me." Reorder your life. Change your priorities. Redefine what your life means.

We should not disconnect the importance of facts. The facts of history are both interesting and very important. The trial of Timothy McVeigh was trying to get at the facts of what happened. The trial was not to get at the truth. The trial was to get at the facts. Facts describe our being here. We must continually expand our almanac of information. But when we get all our facts straight, they will not set us free. The *Encyclopedia Britannica* will not give us hope.

Freedom. The facts will not liberate us. Hear again the strange words of Jesus: "The truth will set us free."

To be honest, you and I long far more for freedom than for truth. We do not often long for truth. Indeed, we often hide from the truth, obscure the truth, lie about the truth.

It is yearning to be free that burns within us. We long for freedom because of the overpowering sense of being in bondage. It is not chains or shackles we fear. I heard no shackles as you came in today. We live in bondage to uncertainty and to fear itself—shackles far more binding than chains. Uncertainty. What happens after college? Where do we go from here? Does she really care for me? Uncertainty. We are paralyzed by fear—the fear that we will be here and no one will notice.

We are bound by ignorance. All of this learning going on around here is scary because it discloses what we do not know.

We live in bondage to prejudice—prejudice toward all those who are different than we. Different color. Different ideas. We are in bondage to our prejudice toward the poor or the rich, toward women or men, toward gays or straights.

We live in bondage to our resentments—people who were recognized while we were left in the shadows, resentment toward someone who hurt us deeply.

We live in bondage to bitterness, bitter because of some broken promise. For all of us, life becomes bruised, our souls black and blue from bumping into one another's harsh words and painful neglect.

That's where we find ourselves. We long more to be free than to be true—to be free of dread and uncertainty, to be free of fear and bitterness.

To be free. And how shall we be free?

We reach for freedom in ways that reflect the best within our souls and we grasp for freedom in ways that diminish the human spirit. The abuse of one another and ourselves through physical violence, so common as to be expected. The violence of drug and alcohol abuse takes place daily. Sexual abuse is growing, not declining. Abuse of those of different sexual orientation is not a sign of holiness. It is a sign of ugliness. We grasp for freedom by denying our human boundaries. We grasp for freedom by enslaving others, making them serve our ideas and priorities.

Excessive claims of power or knowledge or even virtue can become ways of killing and diminishing the human spirit.

The lessons of Holy Scripture teach us to look for freedom not in the accumulation of power or wealth, not even the storing up of knowledge and virtue—surely good things.

To be free—hear this gospel word—to be free means to *become* a person of truth. The truth is not a statement to affirm. The truth is a person to become. You and I are not free when we believe the right things. Right belief will never set us free.

The siren's call to craft a set of right beliefs and hold onto them with all our might is to build and to climb aboard a homemade boat that will be dashed to pieces on the shoals of pain and inexplicable grief. We cannot create vessels of true belief that will free us from dread and disease.

We play games trying to prove that our "truth vessels," our homemade doctrinal boats, are more seaworthy than yours. We should not become enamored by our words. All our creeds and doctrines are temporary vessels for crossing a stretch of life's waters. To be sure we will always make our boats. But they have to be mended again and again because they leak, sometimes dry-docked altogether. Our homemade statements of truth are frail, human-made crafts for sailing on life's turbulent seas. They will never set us free. John Calvin was just a person—so were Peter and John Paul II. They were indeed better shipbuilders than most of us. But they make only human ships. Even with God's help, we make only human ships.

We are not free because we believe the right things or sail in the right doctrinal boats. We become free when we become the right person. Our high calling is to find the truth of our lives. Jesus gives us light by which to see the truth of our being here.

Each one of us is a gift of God to the world. Your high calling and mine is to find the truth of our lives. There and only there lies our freedom, freedom that is free.

Jesus said "The truth shall set you free." And he said again "I am the truth." The truth is not a sermon to believe—not even the Sermon on the Mount. The truth is a person to follow.

The trustworthiness of truth will never lie in what we say. Words will fail us. We cannot utter words—no matter how golden—that will set us free. Our greatest challenge is not to tell the truth. Our higher calling is to be the truth. The truth that sustains and persuades is not the truth we say, but the truth we are.

We cannot build our being together with one another or even with God upon words. Relationships are far more powerful than words. The gospel is not to tell people that God loves them. That is not the gospel. The gospel is to love them on God's behalf. You can't tell the gospel to somebody you don't care about.

The truth that sets us free is a radically transforming human experience. The early disciples discovered that following Jesus changed everything. It changed how they saw their work. It changed how they related to one another. It changed how they understood their religion. It changed their behavior. It changed their priorities. It made brothers out of strangers and strangers out of family.

Hope is the gospel. Embodying the truth will set us free.

It takes great courage to step out of the life rafts of religious doctrine and secular certainty in which we comfortably live and step into the raging waters that seem certain to engulf us, of loving and being despised for it, of forgiving and being ridiculed for it. Yet that is what Jesus invited his stakeholder Peter to do. Go ahead, Peter, step out of the boat into the high waves and the volatile winds. Peter was just crazy enough to do it. It is not that you won't sink. Peter sank. But for Peter, sinking was not the last word.

Embodying the truth, following the truth, walking in the truth in the midst of life's most difficult waters does not mean that we will not sink. It means that we are free to fall without drowning. We are free to fail, without being failures.

Here is the truth that will set you free. God is with us. That truth will set us free from the panic that we have to make it on our own merit or our own knowledge or our own power. We can rest from the panic that our life rafts of doctrine and religion will see us to the shore. They will not. The hope of life is not that we will somehow believe the correct truth. The hope of life is that we will become the truth, that we will follow the truth.

Our calling is akin to that of Peter. It is to trust ourselves to the Truth. Our freedom will not lie in knowing the truth. The gift of freedom lies in the courage to live the truth, the courage to become a person of truth. Jesus said, "I am the truth." Reach for the courage to become the truth and you shall be free indeed.

Amen.

War and Peace

The indignation that has exploded around the world over the devastations in Baghdad and Palestine heightens the world's anxiety and fear. The people of Earth have become a civilization afraid of itself, afraid of its own instincts, afraid of its own commitments, uneasy about its own fragile pacts of peace.

The truth is that we are a warring civilization. We talk of peace but act as warriors. We admonish respect for human life but we behave with disrespect for one another. We lift high the rhetoric of concern, while we wallow in the troughs of turmoil.

Where is the voice of the people of faith in the midst of war? Are we to be silenced by the loud noise of political exchange or are we to be guided by another voice. It becomes plain. Chiefly, you and I are children of the world. We take our clues from the political and social environment, hearing only faintly the call to faith.

Even in our faith we have preferred wrath and judgment to love and redemption. Judgment is closer to where we live than redemption. We are children of conflict and we proclaim the virtues of peace, while we pursue the paths of destruction.

The Christian message of peace is so common to our faith, yet so foreign to our understanding. Our warring wears many faces. We are all the children of Cain and Abel. Cain lives within you and me, glaring at Abel. How shall we kill our brother? Let us count the ways. We kill him with bombs. We kill him with hatred. We kill him with goodness. And we shroud each of our weapons with the guise of peace.

We build missiles for peace, one round of our nation's missiles being known as "The Peacekeeper." Can we be so naïve? War does not bring peace. War exposes the anger and the fear that reigns over us. War is not an American phenomenon or a Russian phenomenon or an Israeli phenomenon or an Iraqi phenomenon. War is a human phenomenon. War reveals the face of fear and uneasiness that corrodes our human living together.

In the deep night, when we look at the starry heavens, we realize that we inhabit such a modest place in the universe. The differences among people on Planet Earth are so trivial. Cain and Abel, Americans and Russians, Iraqi and Israeli spring from the same womb. We fight and maim and kill in order to preserve the status of firstborn, when our real birthright lies in the one we kill.

We build bombs and bomb shelters, strategies and counterstrategies. We search for the impenetrable shield and seek the ultimate weapon—all in the name of peace. We sustain tension and call it détente. We exist in poised conflict and call it the balance of power.

We build the walls of separation higher and higher, walking atop the narrow ridge between order and chaos, hoping that no one will shove us into oblivion. Recently, I saw a window sticker on the back of a car in London that said "Humpty Dumpty was pushed."

We convene in Geneva. There Cain and Abel sit pushing and shoving, conversing upon a wall of hostility discussing how to build a ladder down before someone falls. Peacemaker bombs? It is a fantasy. It is a vanity of vanities. We have only the illusion of peace.

But the raging pursuit of world power is only a reflection of the wrath among us. You and I, Cain and Abel, look for ways to expel one another. We twist and pervert the truth.

Meanness and deceit distort the way we live together. It is no easy task—this living together as Cain and Abel. We want and like different things. We feel different passions, think different thoughts, walk different paths. We feel so distinctly right and remain convinced that the other person's disagreements spring from his or her own sinister nature. So we scheme. We look for ways to discredit. We sow seeds of distrust. Lying in wait to destroy, we admonish brotherhood and we call it peace. It is our way of peace—the peace that we give, the peace where hatred and personal anger lie only slightly behind the façade of courtesy and good manners. You and I are like Cain and Abel, walking in peace, waiting for God to look the other way. War lies deep within us.

Our peace, this human peace, the peace that we would deliver, marches under the face of goodness. After all, look at us—here we are a righteous people, living in accord with the holy principles of Yahweh. We do battle not with God, but with Satan.

You see, there is no warring like religious warring, no hatred like moral hatred. Watch out for the anger of those who possess the truth. The wrath of the righteous knows no limits and leaves only rubble in its wake. It is the righteous that try to purify our world on God's behalf, working to expunge the evil forces from our midst. We war in the name of goodness.

The church has very often found itself to be the ally of war. Even our evangelism takes on the dreadful character of destruction. The war of faith, the war of moralities, each seeking to establish itself as God's anointed. The church, longing to be tapped as God's church, seeks to insure that its own righteousness will prevail. It is a war under the guise of faith. We espouse narrowness and call it religious devotion. We espouse self-preservation and call it denominational purity. We espouse self-centeredness and call it the evangelical spirit. The battlefields of religion are littered with hurt and misery, guilt and loneliness, rendered by the church to be evidence that the truth marches on. You and I make war under the flag of righteousness. We make war and call it holy. We make war and call it jihad. We would create peace by the elimination of the wicked.

Almost unnoticed, Jesus walks among us. His presence is so mysterious. He calls people to the Kingdom of God within and calls for us to be at peace. Not to establish peace, not to defend the peace, but to be at peace. Clearly, Jesus simply doesn't understand where we live. Not the world of Cain and Abel. Not the world of Christians and Muslims. Not the world where the forces of evil must be held in check. Not the world where peace must be enforced with the blades of battle.

Jesus' message is so odd, so strange that it must mostly be regarded as irrelevant, largely unrelated to where we work and live. So foreign are his words that we find ways to distract them into making sense. Surely, if peace is to prevail, we must usher it in.

It is actually the gospel that we cannot tolerate. The reality of grace and forgiveness and peace is transformed into a method of salvation. Jesus' presence offers no scheme of salvation, no arbitrary steps toward becoming faithful. The message of Jesus is to be at peace. God's grace is sufficient. *You are forgiven.* There are no methods or strategies to win the peace, or to warrant forgiveness, or to establish grace. Jesus said,

> Peace is my parting gift to you, my own peace [I give to you], such as the world cannot give. Set your troubled hearts at rest, and banish your fears.
>
> (John 14:27 NEB)

Frankly, we have not been interested. It will not work, we say. But the gospel continues to reverberate through the ages. It is not that we should favor little wars over big ones. It is not that we should cover our warring natures with a façade of goodness, or surround the earth with an impenetrable shield. Jesus addresses himself to us far more plainly. He calls upon us to become bearers of his peace, a peace that is within us, to live out peace in the midst of conflict. He calls upon us not to *create* a force for peace but to *become* a force for peace.

Jesus' words translate into the realities of loving and forgiving and bearing mercy. To be at peace means to bear unconditional love for one another.

We prefer preachments. We prefer to translate the Christian meaning of love into words and doctrines. Yet, the peace Jesus gives calls us not to speak but to listen, to know the quiet divine mystery that dwells in each of us, to see that in Cain rests the very countenance of God. To be at peace means the willingness to find godliness tucked behind the faces of hatefulness. It means to see Christ dwelling in the houses of those who breed death and destruction. We prefer to see with our own spectacles and to translate love as mild cooperation and courtesy. But the love that Jesus brought among us affirms the strong and the weak, the tall and the lowly, the victors and the victims. It knows no boundaries. Love will not permit strife to be the final word.

Listen to our faith. Peace is not the aftermath of conflict. Conflict is never anything more than our attempt to create peace on our own terms.

Listen to our faith.

Peace comes as the power of forgiveness. Forgiveness has become so common. How do we say it: "O.K., I'll forgive you this time, but don't you ever let it happen again." My, how we like to forgive. It makes us feel so secure. Forgiveness becomes the ultimate weapon, leaving a person helpless. It is a way of winning.

Listen to our faith.

Peace springs from the forgiveness that bears the hurt and refuses to be bound by the tragedy. The good news of our faith is that God does not wait for us to repent. God has taken the initiative and forgiven us in spite of our ugliness. God's forgiveness is not a psychological volley for man's repentance. Repentance does not make forgiveness possible; forgiveness makes repentance possible. In all of its absurdity, God simply forgives us. Peace lies in the simplicity of God's presence—it is a gift.

We have made our faith so official and efficient, memorizing the cadence and struggling to walk in perfect step. That is the human way. We prefer to hedge the purity of God's grace with confidence in our own system. And all of this clamor to establish our goodness before God exposes for us that human war lies not chiefly between nations or even between brothers. War lies chiefly within us. We are at war with ourselves. It is inner peace for which we long and our war against one another is only a shadow of the war going on within. The roots of war lie within our own hearts. It is the inner turmoil that erupts, that will not let us rest. We long for peace.

Listen to our faith.

The only issue for us is whether we have the courage to live in the power of God's presence. We think of courage as taking a deep breath and walking boldly into battle against the enemies of right. Our faith calls for us to have courage to live in the peace which Jesus gives. It is the ultimate risk to accept another person as good in spite of his evil deeds. Courage means to become an instrument of peace on the landscape of tragedy.

Our faith causes us to see that war is not something that erupts in Iraq. It erupts in our workshops, and in our offices, and in our classrooms, and in our homes. It issues its ugliness in the daily traffic of our living together here and now.

It is to that turmoil that Jesus comes, speaking of love and forgiveness and peace. And Jesus calls us to have the courage to lay claim to the peace within, to be set free from our killing and maiming, to be set free by the reality that we do indeed live in the arms of God's grace and to listen to our faith and know that only in God's embrace is there ultimate peace.

Amen.

Preaching
in the Baptist Wilderness

Preaching is tough duty. The fields of ministry where preachers have to labor are rarely lush green meadows of waving grain or rippling streams of goodwill and affirmation cascading down the shoals of congregational contentment. Ministers live and work on rugged terrain. Their places are more akin to what we might call the desert wilderness. They may be closer to the image of Moses wandering about on the back slopes of Mt. Horeb after being expelled from the pristine innocence of life in the palace.

I want to remind us that we live and minister in a world of images. We have all learned along the way that our lives of preaching and speaking are chiefly about stirring the imagination—enabling, even inspiring people (and sometimes ourselves) to see their worlds in a different light. Too often, in all our professions, we become trapped by roles that become official, rote, and sterile. Boredom takes hold. For those who sit within the range of our voice or influence, seeing ourselves or the circumstances in which we live in a different light is mostly about being captured by the power of imagination.

The image around which I will frame these remarks turns on the episode along Moses' journey where he is tending his father-in-law's sheep. They were not even his own sheep. Sweating under the brutal desert sun, Moses was trying to lead his sheep to a few scraggly leaves sprouting through the craggy, desolate terrain. And here in this tough, dusty, barren place, Moses comes upon a bush ablaze with fire, and then he hears this startling voice that he is standing on holy ground.

Talk about absurd. This is ridiculous. Here in this godfor-saken, empty barren desert of a mountain, he is told that he is standing on holy ground. Maybe a trout stream or a cool oasis, but to call this stretch of earth holy had to have the ring of hyperbole, if not sheer nonsense.

The truth is that most of us live both our professional and personal lives on a road that runs somewhere between the desert wilderness and the promised land. We go to our church fields, to our pulpits, to our diverse callings often with a sense, or an expectation, or even a hope that we are going to the promised land, a land where we will be affirmed and loved, embraced and encouraged, a land of fulfillment and promise. We arrive to find too often that we have come to land marked by conflict and competition, a land where resent-ments and bitter hostilities lie only half-hidden beneath the façade of Sunday worship. Expectation turns to anxiety, hope turns into silent wondering in the deep night about what on earth have I gotten myself into. We make a quarter turn and run into the reality that we are Baptists in a time when Baptists have become dysfunctional and disoriented. Baptists are adrift.

The Baptist wilderness has become more dense than most—overgrown, dark, a veritable briar-patch of deceit and disappointment. Against the backdrop of Baptist confusion and unpleasant rhetoric, our challenge is to keep alive our own imagination and to stir our people's imagination about the promise of the church.

Like some of you, I have been through the dead heat of Baptist turmoil. I have mourned our losses, been preoccupied by our defeats, and officially been declared a heretic. For a while, frankly, I was nurtured far more by the husks of our feuds and failures than any flickering blaze of hope.

If a new day dawns among Baptists, the highest and best hope for doing so will be in a scattering of churches that take a more direct and human responsibility for speaking the gospel in a new voice. My own journey has taken me beyond the boundaries of Southern Baptists. While I have no quarrel with those who wish to hold onto that mantle as a zone of comfort, they simply do not come up on my screen as a relevant force for bringing light and hope. But, for me, out of the mourning called grief, I have come to the dawning of a new morning.

I believe that never in a century has it been more important for churches or ministries to define their character. Specific, concrete communities of faith must bring their witness to life with their own clear sense of calling. We cannot live off the residue of yesterday's passion. We are specific ministers and churches—where people have names and faces. We preach among people who long to find a holy place and who long to be captured by a holy moment.

In all candor, as a denomination, Baptists are in decay. You and I are left to minister in a desert where Baptist principles have been lost amidst the dust storms of religious hype and party politics.

The desert is a depressing place. For Moses, the desert was a long way from the palaces of Egypt where he grew up. Yet, it was here in this remote and desolate, depressing, and apparently godforsaken place, that Moses saw something that he had never seen before. He was startled, virtually spellbound by a flame that would not go out.

We ought to tuck this truth away. It sometimes takes a barren, deserted place to be able to see.

Perhaps it is time for us to see. Baptists are a tragic sight. Baptists have built temples and palaces grander than any belonging to the Roman Church of the Middle Ages. Baptists have become rich and powerful. Baptists own office towers, publishing houses, and television networks. They have achieved giant corporate status and they wield substantial political clout. Vanity. It is all emptiness. It is one more large denominational power structure, selling indulgences, losing its soul in the grasp for political and corporate power.

But, let's be honest. You and I are not even worried about Baptists. We are mostly like Moses—preoccupied with keeping up our own sheep—making our own choices, coping with our own anxieties, struggling with budgets and programs, worrying about our children, consumed with broken promises and wounded relationships. A broken denomination is not on our mind.

So, you and I face a real danger. In the loss of dignity and good faith in our historical Baptist moorings, we can lose our way, even lose our passion for being the church. After all, our congregations have lived through the years chiefly on surrogate caring. We gave our money and somebody else cared in our name. The idea that we might have to take responsibility for caring is a frightful notion.

We are too busy for that, too busy to care directly. We have sheep to tend.

The challenge for Moses was not really about finding the courage to march back down to Egypt. Living beyond the wilderness for Moses and preaching with power and purpose in the Baptist wilderness for you and me will require seeing a new fire in the desert.

The challenge for Baptists is not to retake the palaces. That is nostalgia. The challenge is to let the palaces go. The challenge is to embrace the desert as the place for seeing new light.

I believe that our question is whether we have the courage to craft congregations of Baptists in the Baptist wasteland who can chart a new course. Unless the soul of Baptists is kept alive in a scattering of congregations of faith, Baptists will not endure as a force for grace and hope in the world. End of story. Baptists will drift into triviality and political posturing, and become a mere footnote in religious history.

So, the question we face as congregations and pastors is whether we can live and minister out here in the Baptist wilderness. Can our churches become blazing light to people who are lost and disillusioned amidst the discordant, ugly sounds of religion?

Religion itself has become one of the chief hazards of faith, causing people to lose sight of God. It is time for us to learn that God is not a possession of Christians or Jews or Muslims. God does not embrace our religions. God embraces our people. Our religions are a stack of stones set together to remind us that we once met God here.

Moses had to lose his religion to find God. Adrift from his religious history, cast out by the religious order, wandering about in the desert of disappointment, Moses saw a light that changed the story of his life.

So, the lesson for Moses and for us is this: the burning bushes are not out there in somebody else's wilderness. They are in your wilderness and mine. A wilderness where ordinary people feel alone and betrayed, where churches are broken and glazed over, where relationships are fractured and frayed. That's where we live. That's where we preach. And if hope blazes up for you and me, it will have to be here in this tough terrain.

Preaching in the Baptist wasteland often leaves us tangled and tired. Our journey through the wilderness will have to be trodden through the rocks and shoals that leave bruises and blisters. But, the crisp, enduring lesson of Moses is for us not to define our lives by the bruises. We cannot define our lives by the blisters and the brokenness.

For goodness sake, the message of Moses is not that trouble isn't painful. His message is certainly not that despair doesn't disrupt what we are doing. The word of God is this: The desert is not the end of the road. Life is more than the scorching sun and the desert rocks. A new future for our preaching must be centered around transforming the desert wilderness, the scorched earth of dread and fear and depression, into a sanctuary of hope. We cannot wait for cool, green pastures, idyllic and pristine. The church has to become the fire of God in ordinary history. We are called to rekindle people's imagination and to empower people to transform their scorched earth into holy ground.

The question is whether we can help people change their places from scorched earth to holy ground. The difference turns out not to be in the ground, but how we walk on it.

Scorched earth. You and I have lived there. It sounds like this: "I will forgive him but he had better never let it happen again." Scorched earth. "He doesn't deserve to be forgiven." Scorched earth. "You can be in our church if you vote right." Scorched earth. That's living in the desert.

Holy Ground. Loving people who don't deserve to be loved. Holy Ground. Embracing people who don't measure up. Holy Ground. Loving people, acting for the good of people you don't even like. Holy Ground. Wrapping the wounds of people you don't even know. Holy Ground. That's living by the light of a fire that will not go out.

A new light among Baptists will blaze up when people have the courage to hear a new sound and we have the courage to speak a new word.

We are not here to shout empty religious slogans or demean one another with trivial Christianity, singing twenty-eight stanzas of "Let Us Behold Him." We are here to open people's eyes to a blazing new light.

We are not here to recite the right religious ideology, or to adopt the right formula for church success. We are here to forgive. We are not here to be consumed by mindless Baptist bickering. We are here to embody the gospel in honest caring.

We are not faith-enforcers, acting like a Gestapo for some misguided form of Calvinism. You and I are here to give flesh and blood to a new way of being together.

We are not here to make sure people recite authorized religious language or make sure that women are subservient to men. We are here to be God's people, without respect to race or gender or sexual orientation.

We are not here to require that people embrace the latest version of orthodoxy. We are here to give people hope. We are here to help people in Jesus' name and to ask questions later.

Preaching with a new voice means realizing that caring, after all, is not something grandiose. It is not a theological proposition. Caring is not a skyscraper. Caring is not even about keeping the church alive at all costs. Caring is a simpler calling. Caring means to heal the sick. Caring means to help the poor. Caring means to shelter the homeless and to teach the ignorant. Caring means setting people free of disease, and freeing them from prejudice. It means looking out for people who are lonely, and taking up for people who are powerless.

Baptists have become intoxicated by their own success. Power and popularity, the rhythms of Saturday night have become the beat of Sunday morning. And while we groove, Jesus slips out the back door unnoticed to go look after the hungry.

Listening to a new voice will cause us to hear a different calling. That new calling is to become the flame of God in the desert of religious decay, bringing water to the thirsty in Jesus' name, pushing back the shadows of ignorance in Jesus' name, calling evil by its name even when it wears the mantle of religion.

In truth, preachers and Baptist college presidents have become timid and afraid. In the wilderness we are tempted to be focused on finding enough scraggly bushes to satisfy one more day's hunger. We are consumed by making one more budget, succeeding one more year. If we hear a new voice, our future must take a different turn. Our calling is to risk the church's life, to risk our ministry, to risk the church's history, for people who have nowhere else to turn.

This, I believe, is the word of the Lord. People don't much need to hear they are loved. They need to be loved. People don't much need to hear that God will forgive them. They need to be forgiven. You see, we are going to meet God when we put our arms around someone who is bent over with grief. We will find God in our words of encouragement to someone who feels beaten down. We will see God in our willingness to listen to somebody who thinks that nobody understands. In other words, the gospel is not to tell people that there is hope. The gospel is for us, you and me, to *become* somebody's hope. And when we become somebody's hope, we have taken our first step from the desert wilderness toward the Promised Land.

The Holy Catholic Church

I confess to you that I believe deeply in and lean heavily on the reality of the Holy Catholic Church. That affirmation may not tell you much about where I stand, but worship is a good place, a very good place, to confess our faith and to try to unravel what our confessions mean.

My word today is simple and straightforward. It is this: Church is what happens when God shows up.

The fact is that we mostly run our worlds—that is, we go to the library, we attend our classes, we grade our papers, we answer our letters and return our calls—without much reference to God or the church. The philosopher, Bishop George Berkeley, may have been right after all: "To be is to be perceived." At least, it may not make any difference that God exists if God doesn't show up in the way we go about our studies and grade our papers and answer our letters.

Perhaps that is good. I rather suspect that God's showing up regularly in our endeavors may often interfere with what we are trying to get done. God's presence can be a terrible nuisance.

A powerful lot of Holy Scripture is about just this matter—what happens when God shows up. God's showing up confuses and startles; it rearranges people's values and their priorities. It turns cultures upside down. Inevitably, God seems to show up at the most inopportune moment, in the strangest setting, and at the most inconvenient time. God simply will not seem to follow our rules for religious practice. It is very difficult to hem God in with our religious systems. When we think we have God under control, God eludes our grasp. God's obvious presence and God's apparent absence can be terribly confusing and frustrating.

Perhaps we can learn from the people of ancient Israel about what it means when God shows up and even a hint of what it means to be the church. There is something familiar about what happened to them in their lonely life of exile in Egypt. On certain occasions, you and I are startled by the unshakable sense that God is in our vicinity.

We may not know what name to give to God's presence—but we are sometimes overcome by a haunting awareness that our lives and our relationships are more than they appear on the surface. I am more than what I say and do. There is an inwardness about our lives—obviously layered over by all of the busyness and noise. But when the noise subsides and the light fades, there is a center to our being—a reason for being here—that is not exhausted by our work or by our words.

The church is what happens when we are compelled by the light of God's presence to look beyond the traffic of our daily activities. Startled and confused though we may be, the church is born in that transforming experience when we see that we are more than the goings and comings that consume our waking hours. We are more than running to work, going to class, winning friends, and laying our head down to rest.

Listen to the writer of Exodus. Listen to the rumble of God's showing up. The writer has God speaking:

> "You have seen what I did . . . how I bore you on eagles' wings and brought you unto myself. Now . . . , if you will obey my voice . . . and keep my covenant, then you shall be a special treasure. . . . [Y]ou shall be unto me a kingdom of priests and a holy nation."
>
> (Exodus 19:4-6)

A "kingdom of priests," a "holy nation"—there is not, even in the New Testament, a better description of the Holy Catholic Church.

Perhaps it sounds a bit odd—at least remote from the language we use every day. Yet, that's what the church is—a kingdom of priests, a cadre of people who see themselves as caregivers, people for whom caring, reaching out, taking hold, lifting up is not just a good deed, but the essential character of what it means to he here. Touching, comforting, forgiving, accepting—it is the work of priests. It is the essence, the only thing that finally matters for people who call themselves the church.

And as regards this matter of a holy nation—people who are set apart, not by arrogance and elitism, but by the power of new centering that takes place in their lives—holiness is not arrogance; it is centeredness. It is a self-understanding that is informed and shaped by God's presence.

A kingdom of priests, a holy nation. That's the reality of the Holy Catholic Church. But the question is how do we get from here to there and what will it do to us when we get there. You see, believing in the church may turn out to be more than we bargained for.

First, how do we get from here to there? It is my hunch that we get there much the same way that Israel got from bondage to freedom. Hear the lesson of Holy Scripture: "You have seen how I bore you on eagles' wings." Freedom is a gift. The freedom from fear is a gift. The freedom to love is a gift. It is called *grace* in the language of faith. Grace means that God reaches out to us and lifts us from the defeat and the depression—not because we want it or demand it or even expect it, but because that is who God is and what God is like.

The Church is built on who God is, what God is like and how God behaves. That stands in stark contrast to building the church on who *we* are, what *we* are like, or how *we* behave. There lies the difference between churches as we experience them—our churches—and the Holy Catholic Church. The Holy Catholic Church is God's Church built on God's reality—the reality of grace, the reality of God's presence in our difficult world, built on the reality of God's coming to be one of us.

Our churches, on the other hand, are human endeavors, frail organizations that try to lay hold of God. Our churches are sometimes simply a cry for the church to happen among us. They are sometimes feeble attempts to cover up the fact that we have abandoned being the people of God, that we have become enamored by our own success at building colorful, big, loud religious organizations.

And yet, our churches sometimes become the church, the Holy Catholic Church, celebrating that God has come to us, that God has set us free, empowering us to become a force for love and grace and hope in a frightened and troubled world.

So, the reality of the Holy Catholic Church is rooted in sheer grace. Its foundation is not in what we have done or in what we feel or even in what we can accomplish. The church is not based on our best instincts or our fondest hopes. The foundation of the church is God's showing up, on eagles' wings or in a manger's bed. God does manage to show up in the strangest places.

Getting from here to there. That may be our most important journey—to go from being a mere collection of worshippers, rather tattered of soul and empty of spirit, to being the church, a community of people who live in the light and who are bearers of grace.

We can be the church only when we believe that God will not walk away from us. Believe it. It is a gift of grace. God is going to stay with us through thick and thin, through failure and success. The word of the church is that God will not abandon us, no matter how awful things become.

Now, you cannot discover the power of the Holy Catholic Church unless you come to be lifted up, as it were, on eagles' wings and live in the light of God's being with us.

That's what the church, this body of Christ, this Church Universal turns out to be. It is a body of people who live together in the light of God's being by our side. Peter says it: we are people called to be light (1 Peter 2:9). And God's showing up as Light to our lives changes the way we do things.

Follow me one more step. Hear the words of that ancient writer: "If you will obey my voice . . . and keep my covenant," you will be that kingdom of priests and that holy nation—which in today's language of confession we call the Holy Catholic Church.

Now, what does this mean—obeying God's voice and keeping God's covenant? Let's not make it too complicated. After all, those Hebrew people were not complicated people with Ph.D.s and law degrees. They were just sheepherders, wandering mostly in the desert plains, eking out a living. And so God tried to spell out what it meant to live as people of God. And what God said has come to be called the "Ten Commandments." They go mostly like this. I have brought you out on eagles wings—an act of grace. What does it mean to live this way? What is "grace-living" like? Grace living means that you take God and your heritage, your mother and father seriously. It means that you respect one another's property, you respect one another's rights, you respect one another's relationships. That's what those ten commandments are about—giving us clues to what living in the light means.

Jesus had a little simpler version of the ten. He just said that "grace living" means loving God with all your heart, soul, mind, and strength, and taking care of each other as you would take care of yourself.

My point is this: Whenever God really shows up in our lives, it makes a difference in how we show up in one another's life.

And what kind of difference does it make? I leave you today with two words.

1. First, being the Holy Catholic Church is not about organizations and hierarchies. It is not about institutions—not about Baptists and Methodists and Roman Catholics.

The first word, rather is this: The church is about meeting each other differently. The church is about meeting each other in a new way. That's the difference it makes.

Being the church causes us to see one another differently—real people—roommates, and parents, and teachers, and students, and colleagues. It causes us to see the world's people differently. To see Israelis, Iraqis, Iranians, Palestinians, South Africans, Afrikaners, Germans, Portuguese, Russians differently. The Holy Catholic church teaches us that these people are all children of God. They are on God's eagles wings. God likes them, God forgives them, God is holding onto them, and God will not let them go.

We are at war. Meeting each other differently means there are no holy wars. Holy war is an oxymoron. All war is unholy. All warriors are people and people are holy. War should cause us to repent, to bind up our wounds and to bind our enemies' wounds. War is always an act of men and women, never an act of God.

What difference does it make that God has shown up to be by our side? The first word is that it changes how we meet each other. Fear becomes love and revenge becomes forgiveness.

2. The second word is this. Being the Holy Catholic Church is about seeing ourselves differently. You and I are people with a center and the greatest gift of faith is to come in touch with that center. Being the church means discovering that God is with us—at our side; that God is for us—when we win or when we lose, when we pass or when we fail; and that God is within us, living grace and hope and forgiveness through us.

So, I believe in the Holy Catholic Church. You and I mostly live scattered lives, moving from one preoccupation to another, from one relationship to another, from one hero to another. Being the church means finding an enduring center, a center that will not be eclipsed. Finding a center, not that we will always live by, but that we can always return to and from which we can gain our bearings.

I believe in the church and I believe that the church is what happens when God shows up. He shows up in Egypt as the wings of an eagle. He shows up in Bethlehem as a baby in a manger. He shows up as Light. I suppose that the church is more like a verb than a noun. The church *happens*. It grips us, engages us, changes us, transforms us, makes us into new people, people who are focused by the centering power of God's presence.

Believe it or not, God has even been known to show up here in the vicinity of the University. It we have the courage to open ourselves to God's embrace, he will set you and me free.

And what will we do with God's gift of freedom? The freedom that is not the absence of a boundary but the presence of a center. What will we do with our freedom?

We will care for each other.

We will live with hope.

We will become the Holy Catholic Church.

Amen.

Lessons on Time

The time has come to think about time. My conviction is that, above all else, you and I must come to grips with the issue of making time our servant and not our master.

Time. We waste time; we save time; we spend time; we lose time; we beat time; we even kill time. We say time drags, that it flies, that it stands still. We buy books we don't have time to read and collect travel brochures for trips we don't have time to take. We bear families we don't have time to see.

Our lives today seem so dominated by the passing of time. It is a bit odd—that though time is significant, it is mostly unreal. An education should be about helping us to distinguish the real from the unreal. But it is clear that we are often dominated by the unrealities in our lives. That we live in time and are therefore its victims seems like only *common sense*. The trouble with common sense is that it is neither *common* nor *sensible*. As Einstein put it, "Common sense is nothing more than a deposit of prejudices laid down in the mind before you reach eighteen."

I remember the staggering impression made on me when the first men journeyed off into space so far that the earth appeared on the horizon as a "blue marble." From that place far away, the differences among us became indistinguishable. No doubt they could recall, in their orbiting silence, the battles taking place on earth that were furious and barbarian. But as these men drifted into the boundless ocean of quietness, the wars lost all their power. Indeed, the battles were no more than feuds among children. From that viewpoint, drifting in space, the tensions and hostilities that are so real and devastating to us became naïve and foolish, almost unreal.

We need to take a similar journey into the meaning of time. If we can back off so that the passage of the years can be viewed as a simple moment, we may become wiser about the time of our lives. We make ourselves frantic. Instead of spending the day doing one thing well, our society presses us to spend it doing twenty things efficiently.

Our days are mostly convenient packages for looking at our experience. We should not delude ourselves into thinking that time is an essential matter. In the end, we are not likely to be known by the number of days we have lived, but by the way we chose to live those days. I judge it even to be a serious distortion of the truth to suggest that we live in time. It would be better to say that time lives in us.

Time is somewhat like space. Space is not something out there that we probe. Space exists only by virtue of the things, and the peoples, and the galaxies, and the stars, and the quasars, and the black holes, and the relationship among these events.

So it is with time. Time is no abstract flow of minutes and seconds and hours. Time is defined by what happens to us and what we cause to happen. You and I are something that has happened in the world. Time is here because of us. Without us, time has no character, it has no color, it has no life, no beginning, and no ending. It is you and I who have character. We have meaning. It is not that we must chase reality before time fleets away. Reality is within us.

In our lives, time has mostly become a burden. We count days and minutes and we number our lives. Time has become our master. We count the years in school and wonder if they will ever end. We count our days on a calendar and if we do, we can only be struck with the fact that some, perhaps most, of our days have gone by.

So, I leave you today with this lesson: the ticking of time is trivial. When the ticking is finished, whether the human clock reads twenty years or eighty years will really not matter much. What will matter will be the pattern of meaning and choices that have marked those years.

My lesson is to suggest that we can live with integrity only if we live beyond the clock. Human problems, human pain, and human values are larger than time. The times change. The enduring issues do not.

The fear of not knowing what step to take.

The human misuse of one another.

The power and pain of suspicion.

The devastation of greed.

That is to say that fear and doubt, malice and anger, are not time-bound phenomena. They are the stuff of human living. Respect and integrity and hope are not time-bound matter. They are the essence of human living.

On this day, learn this lesson: We must not only manage to live longer; you and I somehow must learn to live better. The certainty of one more day will be of little value if we have deluded ourselves into thinking that "one more day" represents the human triumph.

It is your life, your being here, which is the human triumph. Here we are in the midst of a noisy, vibrating world all around us. Yet no one stands where you stand, or sees what you see, or hears what you hear, or even dreams what you dream. There is not another person who lives where you live. Human achievement arises out of listening to that solitude and taking the risk to stand in your own place, to become your own person, to fulfill your own promise. You will have many people standing in line to tell you what to do, where to live, how to speak, and where to stand. It is not important that you come and stand with me; it is important that you learn to stand.

It is important that you are here. No one can replace you. Unless you fulfill your own promise, those promises will simply remain empty on the scene of human history. It may not matter much, but it will matter. Your failure to claim the power of your presence will create a slight wobble in the universe.

Your being here provides the primary clue to what the world is coming to be. Like it or not, we must turn to you. And in our turning, we must accept the work of your own creation. We must accept the communities you will build, the children you will bear, the books you will write, and the friends you will make.

If you live only by time, there will be no human victory because your time will run out. Your clock will stop. Let us learn together that the human triumph lies in our being present to one another as a force for integrity and for tolerance, present as a force for compassion and humanness, a force for hope and respect.

The ancient Preacher said that there was a time to plant and a time to harvest; a time to kill and a time to heal; a time to build and a time to tear down; a time to weep and a time to laugh. The ancient Preacher said that there is a time to love and a time to hate; a time for making war and a time for making peace.

But be clear on this your day, that what you choose to build and what you choose to tear down, what you choose to keep and what you choose to throw away, what you weep about and what makes you laugh, will make the world a different place. It is in such decisions that you will leave your tracks upon the human scene.

I remind you that you are not children of time but that time will be your child. History will be your legacy. Only your choices will endure.

We live in a tangled world that you and I bear the burden for untangling. The tragedy of life is not death; it is what dies within us while we live. Therefore, the real measure of your life will not be in how far you can run, or how high you can leap, or even how long you can live. The real measure will be in whether you think straight, whether you act with dignity and civility, whether you are willing to become a force for hope in the world.

Time. Save it, spend it, kill it. Your job and mine is to redeem it.

Beginning at Home

All three of the Synoptic Gospels tell the story of Jesus coming home. Nazareth was the small town where Jesus grew up—the place where he played sandlot football, where he came home with muddy clothes and dirt in his eyes. Nazareth was the place where he scuffled and argued with his brothers, tore his britches climbing the craggy terrain, the place where he learned to read and write. It was the place where he tagged along with his mother to the market and where he watched his carpenter father, Joseph, and learned to saw a straight line and plumb the corner of a house. There Joseph and Mary took him to synagogue on Sabbath days. He heard the Torah read and learned the law of Moses. So, from dusty paths of children's play to the hallowed places called synagogue, Jesus grew up in this small town called Nazareth.

Nazareth was pretty much like your town—Dublin, Cornelia, McRae, Bremen, Blythe, Duluth. It was an ordinary town. There was a town market, a schoolhouse, a church house, and dusty roads. It had no sanctimonious feel to it—no more than Macon or Milledgeville. It was a poor village—no factories, no Wal-Marts. It was a simple village for living and eking out a daily living together. It was a common place.

And Jesus, well, he was an ordinary youngster—wanting to stay up past bedtime, grubby and bruised from playing hard, captivated by what he was learning at the synagogue and school.

The storyteller, Luke, probably gives us the most descriptive story of Jesus coming home (Luke 4:16-30). Jesus came home to Nazareth immediately after being in that remote, barren place we call "wilderness." Now, most of us have been to the wilderness. It is a place of dread and doubt, a place of uncertainty and unease. It is usually not a place that is far away. Many people run into forty days and nights of wilderness while they are away in college.

What on earth was Jesus doing in the wilderness? Like you and me, Jesus was trying to figure out what he was going to be when he grew up. He lost himself in the wilderness and faced up to some of the alternatives that lay before him. Pulled in different directions, we often have to find some space, to elude the noise, to meet ourselves and to redefine our connection to God.

Jesus wrestled with the urge to pursue other careers—to make something of himself that would bring him more acclaim in his hometown. We all want to do well in our hometown. Out there in the wilderness, Jesus left aside family and friends. He was alone. We would probably describe his state as a kind of classical depression. We often give the wilderness a sterile name. But out there alone, Jesus was deeply depressed. He didn't eat. He was alone as the dark shadows of night crept in over the barren rocks.

It takes genuine courage to face up to the uncertainty in our lives. Frankly, it is usually easier to keep the noise going. Jesus wandered and he wondered, what was to come of him? He could pursue plain old financial success. Bread, we call it. He could pursue status, stations of authority and power or the fortunes of fame. Jesus could pursue political power. Jesus was torn in many directions. So are we. The irrational, the selfish, the draw of stardom haunts us. Oh, there really is a devil. He is not a god tempting us from without. The Evil One is not coming at us with forks and fire. The tempter's call beckons us to climb the mountains of fame and honor, leaving the valleys of wilderness and uncertainty.

Out of the deep night of wrestling with his own reason for being here, Jesus set his eyes resolutely toward his own sense of purpose. He left the wilderness to walk a road that would ultimately lead him from Galilee to Jerusalem. But he could not go far down that road without facing his own people. His journey began at home.

One of the almost universal experiences of going away to college is how quickly we see the blindness and the ignorance of people back home. We somehow feel like we have risen above them. They seem so out of touch. Even so, in the recesses of every soul is lodged the sights and sounds of home. You see, none of us is homeless. Home may not be where we shall live and work, but our journey to our Jerusalem, to our destiny, usually begins at home.

Just as surely as Jesus lived in Nazareth, Nazareth lived in Jesus. There was no way Jesus could face the tragedy or the triumph of Jerusalem without facing into Nazareth, the place where he had played and gotten into mischief as a little boy.

We should listen up. Everybody has their Nazareth. The ordinary places that leave extraordinary marks upon us. Going back can be a scary trip to make. It sometimes means facing up to prejudice that shaped our lives. It means staring down the bad religion that taught us about a god that does not exist. It means living beyond expectations of being Joseph's boy.

There are lots of ways of relating to home. One way is to spend our lives chasing after the affirmation of the people there.

We see ourselves trying over and over again to hear the homefolk say, "You have done well." One way is to try to add our name to the sign—to hang out a shingle at home that says, "Jones & Jones, Attorneys-at-Law." We sometimes find ourselves trying to live again, not the lives, but the myths of our father and mother. Life for Jesus and for you and me is not about living other people's myths. Our life is about creating and living a new word—a new myth, writing a new story.

Another way of relating to home is to vow never to return. Home is not a place to abandon. There is no wisdom in running away. We have this urge to say, in spirit if not in words, to our parents and brothers and sisters, "I'm out of here." Run as fast as we can run. Go as far as we can go. We can never escape our Nazareth because it is lodged deep within our souls.

The lesson of Jesus is to screw up the courage to come home to Nazareth. If you cannot face who you are with family, you will spend your life on the run. The lesson is not that you will always stay there or chase after their dream for you. The lesson is this: Unless you can meet God in Nazareth, you won't be able to hear God in Jerusalem.

When Jesus came to Nazareth, he no doubt did what he was accustomed to doing. People paid little attention when he dropped by to see old school friends and came by the shop as they were working away on a new set of benches.

Then he went to church. People looked up when they handed him the book to read in the synagogue. Everything was going fine until Jesus sat down and began to speak. Friends and family in this small synagogue were tired from a long, hot week of work. Finally, Friday Sundown comes. It is time to rest. The last thing they wanted to hear was a challenge to their comfortable faith. It was the custom in the Jewish synagogue that you stood up to read Holy Scripture and you sat down to preach.

So, Jesus sat down. By this time, Jesus had their attention. Hometown Boy. Rumors were that he was doing some unusual things around the countryside. The room was quiet, people were straining to hear what he might say. The first word that Luke recorded that Jesus said was "Today." He didn't begin slowly saying I remember growing up here. He began by linking the word of Isaiah to that very moment in their personal histories and by startling the congregation.

Jesus spoke plainly of the overpowering sense that our calling is not so much to worship in our synagogue, but to heal the brokenhearted, to deliver people from the chains in which they live, to set people free. It was a stunning announcement. Their response was entirely predictable. "Hey, is that Joseph's boy?"

You can be sure of this. Jesus learned that day that the people who know you best are sometimes the people who understand you least. They bring to their relationship with you a long history. They can't let go of their history. When Jesus responded to their confusion by saying, "No prophet is accepted in his own country," he was not saying that you cannot go back home. He was saying something more powerful: the perceptions of us by family and friends, by classmates and childhood lovers, does not alone define who we are.

Each of us is a special word from God. Having the courage to hear the sounds that only you can hear, to see the truth that only you can see, to deliver the captives that only you can deliver, to heal the broken hearts that only you can heal, having the courage to embrace your gifts does not mean leaving home. It means going back home. It means transforming the meaning of home. Our calling is not to leave home every time we are out of step but to challenge home to walk to a new cadence.

Jesus set before his family and friends a wider, more-embracing vision of God. He reminded them that God was not a possession of Jews or Christians. We like to keep God in our own religious camp. Jesus remembered that when the famines came, God's first visit was not to Israel. God's first visit was to a Phoenician woman—a foreigner. When the land was troubled with disease, it was not to the Jews that hope was first born. It was to a Syrian man named Naaman. Home is the place of the expected and the familiar. Jesus reminded them that God does the unexpected. God reaches out to embrace the forgotten.

To say the least, Jesus' friends were annoyed with him. They grew up with one set of boundaries, and Jesus seemed to be moving them. In order to protect the civil order and to preserve the church, they decided they had better expel this young renegade before he made trouble in Nazareth. So, "passing through the midst of them, Jesus went his way."

We should understand, of course, that Jesus could have stayed in Nazareth, and built houses there with the Joseph and Joshua Construction Company. He could have gone to the synagogue on the sabbath, and perhaps lived to be about eighty-five. Surely, Jesus himself must have found remaining there a compelling alternative. Instead, he walked toward uncertainty. He followed a light and a pathway without knowing where it would lead him. So here we are today still listening to the echoes of his way as we try to find our way from our Nazareth to our Jerusalem.

Listen to the strange sounds of his words shortly after leaving Nazareth.

Blessed are you poor. God's whole world is yours. . . .
Blessed are you who weep now. Weeping will not be the last word. You will laugh again.
Blessed are you even when people hate you or exclude you or kick you out. There will be a new day and you will leap for joy. . . .

"Jesus went *his* way." Listen to the echoes of his way.

Love your enemies. It is easy enough to pay attention to those who love you. I say do good to those who don't like you, who intend you harm. Don't do them good hoping for something in return. Do them good because that's God's way.

If someone hits you, don't live your life trying to get even. Let the score be uneven.

These are strange sounds in a world where children are killing children, in Pennsylvania, and in Arkansas, and in Mississippi, and in Minnesota. These are strange sounds in a world where we make war to protect oil, where we expect to overcome capital crimes with capital punishment—where we expect to stop killing with more killing.

These are strange words in a world where religious denominations accept and exclude people on the basis of race and sexual orientation, where the church can lead the way in being mean-spirited.

Our homegrown doctrines and practices feel good and comfortable. We grew up with those practices. They seem right. But the gospel always changes how home is lived out in our lives.

Well, here you are about to go home. Don't be afraid. Home belongs to your soul. But take with you these lessons from Jesus.

1. Don't ever forget where you are from. Make that connection. College and marriage and careers and relationships will take you beyond home but Nazareth is lodged in your soul.

2. Find a way to mark that place with the gift of gratitude. They held you, healed your bruises, and loved you even when you were hard to love. Gratitude is the best sign of growing up.

3. Home is a good place to look more deeply into your own soul. It is a good place to seek solitude—maybe even to go into the wilderness, to chart a course that embodies who you are, what you see, the sounds you hear, the gifts you bring to the world.

4. Our life is not about chasing after home's approval or running away. It is about learning to walk there with integrity. Integrity means walking in old places with new light. But as we walk, let us learn to hold onto our history because we always find our history in our future. Home is a good place to begin your journey toward your Jerusalem.

Amen.

Easu Is Coming

In the book of Genesis, we find the story of a dreadful meeting, the meeting of Jacob and Esau. I suspect all of us have had dreadful meetings—a meeting we knew we had to have even though we were filled with dread. We can identify with Jacob, who was having to come face to face with his brother Esau. The writer of Genesis sets the scene.

> Then Jacob was greatly afraid and distressed. . . .
> "Deliver me, I pray thee, from the hand of my brother,
> from the hand of Esau." . . . And he got up that night
> and took his two wives and his two handmaids and his
> eleven children and crossed over the river called
> Jabbok. . . . And Jacob was left alone. Someone
> wrestled with him there till daybreak. . . . Then he
> said, "Your name shall no more be called Jacob, but
> Israel, for you have striven with God and with men
> and you have prevailed." . . . And as he passed over
> Penial, the sun rose upon him and he limped.
>
> (Genesis 32:6-32)

The Church today doesn't know much about dread. The church has become a huge success. The pews are packed. The television cameras peer into the pulpit. Churches are collecting more revenues and they are becoming more spectacular than ever before. Worship has become a major production.

Preaching has become stardom. We climb into the pulpit. A hush falls over the waiting congregation. They are waiting for a word. The music has faded. The announcements are finished. The gospels have been read. In the front pew an elderly woman turns up her hearing aid—waiting for a word. A young woman slips her six year old a lifesaver and a magic marker, so she can listen for a word. A college sophomore, home for the weekend, slumps forward with his chin in his hand, doubtful that he will be interested. The vice president of the bank, who has seriously considered quitting his job this week, places his hymnal in the rack, his spirit racked with anxiety, waiting. His wife creases the bulletin in the center and tucks it in her purse. Everybody is waiting.

There we are—God's preachers. There are all sorts of pressures on us to be colorful. We have about ninety seconds to bring a word or else we know they will leave us to ponder the pieces of their lives that do not fit. We have pressures to be contemporary, pressures to be relevant, pressures to be engaging. We have pressures to bring answers to a world that is already full of answers.

People today are looking and finding answers everywhere. Meditation is an answer. Politics is an answer. Aerobics is an answer. Robert Schuler is an answer. Benny Hinn is an answer. Rick Warren's Saddleback theology is an answer. Gingko Biloba is an answer. Acupuncture is an answer. Natural food, yogurt, and brown rice are answers. There are lots of answers. So, why should we be heard?

The pressure is on and everybody waits. They wonder if God is going to show up here in this neighborhood.

The truth is, we all live in pressure cookers. Like Jacob, we probably do not even notice the pressure building. We are on a tear—making it big. We are trying to keep up with the beat, trying to climb one more mountain, trying to stretch one more budget, trying to smooth over one more crumpled relationship, trying to act serene and undisturbed one more time even when we are scared to death.

Then there comes Esau, riding toward us. Oh God, why now? I don't know the name of your Esau, or what horse he is riding, but I know that Esau is coming. It was not the Esau that was outside Jacob that was Jacob's greatest terror. It was the Esau within Jacob. The Esaus within are always the greatest terror. The Esau within brings the pressure and the guilt of the burden. The Esau of guilt and loneliness and fear thunders toward Jacob just as our Esaus thunder toward us. Esau wears so many faces and rides so many horses. The faces of Esau cause us to wonder if we will ever get our lives together, if there really is hope. Wondering about children killing children, bombs killing innocents. We live amidst this strange mixture of fear and confidence.

Watch Jacob drift back over the Jabbok, uncertainty gripping every step. Feel the pain and watch the fear. Sense the uneasiness that causes a chill to run over him. For Jacob, it has been run, rabbit, run. Deal, brother, deal. Preach, sister, preach. Run until exhaustion and regret and remorse overtake us. Listen to Jacob's steps as he drops powerless toward the bare earth. Listen and we can hear the echo of our own steps, our own aches, our own uneasiness.

The silence of the dark night can be a frightening thing. We are mostly consumed by the sounds of escalators and traffic jams, the cries of children, and the ring of commerce. And, when we are left alone in the dark night, we sometimes grow afraid because we can't help but remember that Esau is coming.

This dreadful silence is the birthplace of prayer. It is that place where we can discover that prayer is more about listening than speaking, more about stumbling for words than eloquence.

So, prayer should not be confused with speaking words. We already talk too much. When Esau is on his way, words seem so frail. Whatever else prayer means, the call to unceasing prayer is not a call to talk. It is more likely a call to listen. To "pray always" is far more an admonition to listen to God. We have forgotten how to be quiet. We love the noise. If we want to pray, we have to be prepared to go back across the river and be alone in utter silence and utter darkness. Esau is coming.

Facing up to the reality that Esau is coming is the first step toward the Promised Land. That's when we begin to pray—when we expose all our uncertainties, all our fears. We face into the dread. We confess our real situation, ready for God to see us the way we really are.

We cannot pray unless we are ready for that sort of vulnerability. You see, pretense is the antipathy of prayer. Prayer can become one more attempt to disguise ourselves. It is not that we do not want to speak to God. It is that we do not want to be naked before God. Consumed by the fact that Esau is coming, we face God with all our pretenses shattered. Party time is over. It is time to sweat.

So, prayer is a means of leveling with God. It means radical honesty. We prefer to select our words with such care. We craft prayer that will warrant God's pleasure. The truth is that prayer for us, like prayer for Jacob, is more likely to happen when we have given up on praying.

Prayer turns out to be the first step of putting things in their right order. Prayer does not put things right. Prayer puts things in the right order. When we level with God, we acknowledge our own weakness. We admit our own ignorance. We confess our own fear. Acknowledging our weakness is the beginning of strength. Admitting our ignorance is the foundation of wisdom. And confessing our fear is the basis of hope.

When life really gets difficult and we find ourselves in an inescapable corner, we inevitably pray. No one tells us to pray. Prayer erupts within us. When we are at our wits end, we crumple up in prayer. We beg for a way out. There is not a one of us here who does not know what it means to feel utterly helpless. The confession of our utter helplessness is the beginning of authentic praying. We do not try to frame our feelings of despair in the right words. We do not even know the right words to say. Prayer exposes our deepest hurt. Esau is on his way.

When Esau is coming, the truth is, we long for a miracle. We long for Esau to stumble or to change his mind or for a storm to turn him back. We long for some intervention to our trouble. Some escape from being cornered.

Escape is what we want. There are indeed great moments of escape and cure. Sometimes Esau does turn back for a time. Sometimes there is remission. These mysteries should not be discounted. Our knowledge of human affairs, not to speak of human disease, is terribly limited. But, this I believe: God is not capricious, sometimes listening, sometimes not; sometimes merciful, sometimes not. God does not dip into history on a whim or lift the vale of trauma like an arbitrary visitor. God does not play games with our hearts.

When prayers and miracles are defined as the arbitrary intervention of a remote God whose fancy we hope to catch, we are likely to be disillusioned.

Prayer is not a way of manipulating a particular outcome. We long for a particular outcome. We want our way to be God's way.

So, prayer is not mostly about persuading Esau not to come. It is about meeting Esau in a new way. Prayer transforms our history from victim to creator. That transformation sometimes means healing. Another time it will mean facing loss, even death and tragedy, with the courage to endure. Prayer tunes our hearts to God's grace and grace always, always, changes the meaning of our lives.

Prayer is about crossing back over the river from our traffic jams and commerce. It means facing into the hard lessons we have to learn. The fact is, we do not have all the answers to life neatly tied together in a bright package. The sacrament of silence, crossing back over the river, is for those of us who do not have all the answers. The sacrament of silence is for those of us who sometimes wonder why we are here at all. It is for those of us whose joy is punctuated with real grief. It is for those of us who live patched lives and whose struggle to achieve sometimes leaves us weak and tattered. Silence across the river is for Jacob and it is for me and for you.

Meeting God on the bare, craggy terrain teaches us that beneath our pretensions, beneath our reputations, beneath all our ecclesiastical successes, we are all broken and naked. If we are to meet God, that is where we have to begin.

Meeting God is always about stumbling to an altar. It is about crossing back over the river and laying ourselves open to God with all our vulnerability and uncertainty. It is about wrestling through the night to wrench out the courage to face Esau.

Our Esaus have so many names. They ride so many horses. It may be the Esau of despair, over goals unachieved, deep disappointments that left us crushed, or losses that will not let us go. Esau may ride the stallion of bitterness that causes us to harbor the hurt, holding on to our resentment until it corrodes our spirits and weighs us down. Esau may wear the face of aging parents whose needs outstrip our emotional energies. Esau sometimes meets us on the wild horses of deadly disease and crippled bodies. Sometimes Esau

rips across the stage of our history snuffing out the innocent lives of young school children who thought no trouble would disturb their joy.

In every case, wrestling through the night to find the courage to face into the crippling despair is a journey that changes us forever. In meeting Esau, Jacob's name was changed from Jacob to Israel. Columbine will change its name. Littleton, Colorado will never be the same. The courage to face a new day changes our names and leaves us with a limp. The word from Jacob's limping is that trouble leaves its mark. It always does. We live in the kind of world where people can be hateful to each other, where diseases invade, where people's physical lives deteriorate and where people bomb clinics and towers in the name of God. Where ethnic cleansing seems a sterile description of people killing people.

To endure never means to deny the hurt. There is a more important word. The word is courage. Courage means that the night is not the end of the day.

The lesson of Israel is that meeting Esau is not the end of the journey. The worst thing that happens to us is never the last thing that happens to us.

The charging horses of Esau ride into your life and mine. And, in the sound of the distant thundering threat, we discover the truth about ourselves—that we do not know enough, we are not good enough or strong enough, to stand alone. It is time to learn the truth that going across the river of fear is to cross the threshold of hope.

Prayer is mostly about hope. There was no going around Esau. There never is. But, meeting Esau, facing up to Esau, turns out to be the only way to a land of hope and promise.

Amen.

Learning to Forgive

Human brokenness takes every shape. We are masters of the distorting and twisting of human life. We are all broken people.

On our human journeys, we all need to experience forgiveness. We do not need to understand forgiveness as an idea; we need to experience the power of facing a mistake and being loved anyhow.

Theology is irrelevant to everyday living. Hurt is not. A theological definition of forgiveness largely is irrelevant. Forgiveness is not. The Christian faith, if it matters at all, makes sense only if it touches us where we live.

Pain is a very intimate matter. Theologically, pain doesn't hurt. Theologically, forgiveness doesn't help. Frankly, I worry about the distance between our faith and our living.

Life often hurts. The joys of living are punctuated by moments of real grief and genuine despair. Sometimes we want to run away, to disappear, so that no one will ask who we are or how we feel. We just hurt. And when life is twisted, no amount of talk will dissuade the feeling. Every soul has its dark nights and its deep sense of loneliness. It is during those times when we breathe with a sigh, that we are driven to the inner quiet that calls on the deeper resources of the life we have. And it may be in those speechless interludes that we know ourselves, and it breaks through that we belong to God. When we are in the dungeons of despair, it seems that the light will never break, but the truth of our faith is that the light has broken. We have only to turn toward it. The light is here.

Only if you have hurt can you know the power and meaning of forgiveness. This, I believe, was the point of Jesus in his parable about forgiveness. The force of forgiveness is related directly to the depth of our pain. If you haven't bent with grief, you can't leap for joy.

Forgiveness is a deeply human need. You and I need to know the power of forgiveness, but we have hedged. We have defined and restricted until its meaning has been garbled. We have lost sight of simple forgiveness. In short, we have made forgiveness possible—but only barely.

We have a habit of wanting God to conform to our own image. We make God like us. We want God to think like us and act like us. Nowhere is this clearer than in our understanding of forgiveness. Forgiveness in Christian interpretation has come to be seen as the result of our repentance. God will forgive if we will repent. Hear this word. Repentance does not make forgiveness possible; forgiveness makes repentance possible. God forgives you so that you can look a new way. Conditioned forgiveness is our way of carrying on—not God's way. God forgives—no conditions, no holding back, no time reference at all. Forgiveness is what God is about. Forgiveness is the eternal character of God.

Conditional forgiveness is no forgiveness at all. We all want to hear the other say, "I'm sorry." But that means we don't really want to forgive. Rather, we want our hostility and anger to be justified. Can you see how we have distorted our life together? We play games of getting even and hitting back. We forgive with an air of condescension so as to further cripple the one who has asked forgiveness. In short, we will forgive if he will show us his sorrow and promise not to do it again. We require the full show of sackcloth and ashes. Or we say, "I wouldn't forgive him if he crawled to me on his knees." "Okay, then, I'll forgive you this time." "Well, just don't let it happen again." All these reservations make mockery of the words, "I forgive."

Forgiveness means far more than forgetting. In the act of forgiveness, God does not pretend the transgression never occurred. Rather, God accepts the unacceptable. God forgives in spite of—in spite of—that's the point! More than to forget, it means to remember and move beyond to a higher level of reconciliation. It is this character of forgiveness that seeks to restore a broken or damaged relationship to a new level. In human life, it means not to reclaim an old way of seeing each other, but to move to a new one.

There is never any way of going back to the way things used to be. All such attempts flounder in the sea of self-pity and futile fantasy. Life doesn't go back. It goes forward. But there can be a new day and a fresh relationship. It is that new day that we need. Our hope never rests in the recovery of the "good old days." It rests in the courage to affirm a new meeting between people, the courage to struggle for that new meeting between people, the courage to struggle for that new understanding of each other. We should not try to return to the garden. Our calling is to look toward a new creation, toward a new spirit, toward a new being. That is the only way we can really forgive each other—if we are prepared for a new spirit to take hold of us.

To move beyond not behind, not around but through, the moments of hurt to transcend the occasions of pain; to move through the wounded condition to search for a relationship that remembers the pain but pledges not to be bound by it—this kind of forgiveness is very difficult to realize, because we long for the security of the past. And in asking for forgiveness, we are often asking for things to be like they were. In that case, we don't want forgiveness to occur. We want to retreat.

In our religious lives we usually want to contribute something to God's forgiveness. We want to be faithful in the church or regular in Bible reading or a 100% Sunday school Christian, or something. Somehow, we figure God needs a hand, and so we have our religiously approved methods of helping God forgive us. And, of course, if we can't do something positive, like attend church, we try something negative, such as self-rejection or self-accusation. We punish ourselves in an effort to expunge our guilt and deserve God's forgiveness. Oh, how we work at it!

Guilt is a wrong response to our problems. You know the pain and frustration of feeling guilty. Guilt is a way of turning our backs on ourselves. It is a means of self-rejection. It means saying to ourselves, "I don't like you." But it is the wrong way. It does not solve the problem; it simply drives it within. Guilt is debilitating and destructive. It can cause us to crumble under our own weight.

Self-hatred is a common means of trying to warrant God's forgiveness. This inner hostility often breaks out as either bitter arrogance or cynical harshness. The lesson of grace is to learn to love ourselves as God loves us. When we see the presence of God within ourselves, self-hatred begins to melt away. Inner hostility gives way to inner respect and the confidence that is born of seeing ourselves as children of God.

Where we have not accepted God's forgiveness, there is always a clue. You know it. The clue is that we can't forgive. We harbor the hurt and nourish it and hold on to it for our salvation. As long as we feel rejected, we will reject. But if we ever feel the divine acceptance which holds us, life can break forth again. We are set free.

The need to experience forgiveness is fundamental to our living together. Even the self-righteous want forgiveness, but they believe they don't need much. But those who have found a deep sense of God's forgiveness are able to love and forgive with a growing freedom, and the barriers that stand between them and others begin to break down. Overcoming estrangement is so important to life that we cannot delay. Let me suggest some ways of climbing over the walls that separate us.

1. We must learn to look for the good in each other. Hostility breeds strife and inner discontent. The hateful acts of the estranged never express all that that person is. Our words and our acts toward each other are always ambiguous. But we have to see beyond the ambiguity to the capacity for love and meaning. We must learn to look for the good.

2. We should confront issues that divide us. It is far easier to look away when he approaches, but in that way there is less hope. There is no hope in not speaking, or in wishing the other did not exist. For he does exist, and if life becomes good, it must include the reality of the estranged.

3. Hurt and forgiveness are mutual experiences. There is no solitary suffering or isolated joy. Hurt twists and perverts our own life. Let us meet each other straightforwardly, for only with that honesty can we act to heal the wounds that are taking life from us. Forgiveness can never be accomplished alone. It is a journey for two.

4. Finally, we must not confuse forgiveness with giving in. "Giving in" is weak and this confusion has sometimes made us regard forgiveness as weakness. But true forgiveness takes the greatest strength of all, because it means to take the other's wrong upon us. We bear it together and reach for a new beginning. We will learn to forgive insofar as we believe that we have been forgiven.

Our sense of guilt tells us that we need some help with life. But there is good news. We are forgiven! All that remains is to live as if it is so. Living as if it is so is to take one more step toward the new creation. If Jesus had not said, "Father, forgive them," he could not have lived beyond the grave. Forgiveness sets us free, even from death and hurt. If you believe you are forgiven, act as if it were so.

Amen.

The Plague of Certainty

On a human landscape that has been radically altered by the rise of terrorism, we live and minister in a world that lies more than ever in the frantic grips of uncertainty. From nuclear tests in North Korea and Iran to mindless beheadings in Baghdad, uncertainty reigns.

Our nation is divided and troubled. In all candor, the security, the safety, the certainty of the American way has been an illusion for generations. This illusion was dispelled by nineteen men with box cutters who put our nation in a tailspin. Our response has been a display of power. Even so, here at the height of American power, we would be wise to look out from our lofty perches and see the signs of inner decay that are eroding the American spirit.

The balance of human power, the balance of economic and moral leadership, may be shifting. And in these shifting human sands, the priority and superiority of the Christian religion is beginning to crumble under the might of its internal conflicts and its self-indulgent disputes. We have grown uncertain of our old ways of doing religion.

The world no longer trusts Christians to be Christian. The world has watched us confuse our Christian rhetoric with the preservation of our Western culture. We have allowed the Christian religion to become captive to a horde of Bible-thumping, chorus-singing, homophobic, commandment-worshipping, fast-talking, fundamentalist bullies with Bibles who have alliterated answers for all of life's deepest ills. It is bad religion.

As ministers, we have been conditioned to think that we are supposed to ride in with the right answers wherever trouble exists. We have been trained to think our job is to rub the salve of certainty on the wounds of uncertainty. After all, we are God's priests. We understand God. We know God's way. We know what Jesus would do.

I call it the plague of certainty. We are certain about God, certain about theology, certain about heaven and hell, certain about homosexuality, and certain that Muslims are wrong, certain that war is holy, certain that God is a Christian.

Our certainty is mostly pretense. I believe we will confess our faith more clearly and minister with greater integrity if we can find the courage to confess our uncertainty. Flannery O'Connor was right when she said, "Don't expect faith to clear things up for you. It is trust, not certainty."

Facing squarely into the winds of anxiety, let me offer there images for ministering in this age of deep and profound uncertainty.

First is the image of Jacob having to come face to face with his brother Esau. It is the image of dread—awful, soul-numbing dread. Jacob was consumed, being eaten alive, by dread.

The church today doesn't want to talk much about dread. Yet, this Esau of dread and uncertainty is riding toward most of the people in your congregation. And to make it worse, Esau is riding toward you and me as well. Preachers live in a pressure cooker. Preaching is a dreadful profession. You have pressures to be relevant, pressures to be engaging, pressures to know the right thing to say. You have pressures to be colorful and clever and sure. And all the while, you are often scared to death of the Esaus that are thundering toward you.

I don't know the name of your Esau or what horse he is riding, but I do know that Esau is coming. And, it is not always the Esaus outside that create the greatest fear.

Sometimes it is the Esaus within. They are often the greatest terror—guilt and remorse and isolation. Esau wears so many faces and rides so many horses.

And in the face of dread, our word to those who are waiting for a word Sunday after Sunday, cannot be that Esau is not really out there. Our word, if we have a word, must be spoken by walking back into the darkness with the brokenhearted, going back across the river with them, walking into the deep night with them. We must be willing to wrestle alongside them with the relentless pressures of the fears and the uncertainties that are racking their spirits.

You see, the aim of our preaching cannot be to fix things. Preaching cannot and does not turn Esau away. Preaching doesn't restore certainty. But preaching can change how people are able to meet their Esau. While we should not delude people into thinking that Esau is not really coming, your calling and mine is to change the meaning and the power of Esau's coming. So, the challenge of preaching will not be to vanquish the uncertainty or to eliminate the dread. We need an image of preaching that enables us to become God's angels wrestling in the deep night, helping people find the courage to meet Esau face to face.

A second image about preaching. (This image of preaching comes not from the Bible but from Charlie Brown. You take the truth wherever you find it.) A *Peanuts* cartoon has Lucy at her five-cent counseling booth, where Charlie Brown has stopped to ask advice about life.

Lucy proclaims, "Life is like a deck chair, Charlie Brown. On the great cruise ship of life, some people place their chair at the rear of the ship so they can see where they've been. Others are at the front so they can see where they are going."

The good "doctor" looks at her puzzled client and asks, "On the cruise ship of life, which way is your deck chair facing?"

Without hesitation Charlie Brown replies, glumly, "I can't even get my deck chair unfolded."

Most of our congregants cannot even get their deck chairs unfolded. The winds are too strong. Their ship deck is tossing to and fro and they are just trying desperately to keep their balance.

Michael Yaconelli wrote a little book entitled *Messy Spirituality*. That's where we live. Our spiritual lives are not clean and tidy. The life of the spirit for every one of your parishioners must begin where they are now in the mess of their lives. Accepting the reality of our broken, flawed lives is the beginning of spirituality. The spiritual life will not remove the flaws. Our challenge is to help people let God be present even in the tangledness and the crumpled pages of their lives.

The life of the spirit is complex and complicated and perplexing. Struggling to be Christian today is not an even, straight line toward a life of sure clarity. The Christian life at its best is life under construction, with all of the ups and downs. It has unexpected turns and bumps in the roads and even a few bone-shattering crashes. We are all rough-hewn. We are works in progress, still putting our spiritual lives together, undergirding one another as we cope with he high winds and rough seas.

Being spiritual is not about putting on the make-believe clothing of certainty to wear through the storm. Growing in the spirit is about trusting God in the midst of the storms of uncertainty. Our job as ministers is not to worry about whether people's deck chairs are facing the right direction. Our job is to hand them a chair to hold on to.

A third image is far from Jacob's dread, far from Charlie Brown's deck chair. It is a story from the life of Carlyle Marney, one of us, a man who dared to climb into the pulpit Sunday after Sunday. I do not know whether the story is true but it is a tale that fits the man. Carlyle Marney was a gifted orator, a man who could cast out demons, but like some of us, he could not defeat his own demons. He may be the most powerful preacher that I ever heard—profound, sanctified, dripping with the tones of God, full of energy and pathos, deeply prophetic and profoundly intimate.

The story is told that while he was a senior minister of this stately, high church of a church in Charlotte, Myers Park, that he lumbered into the sanctuary about the time the chancel choir finished an anthem that filled the sanctuary with expectation. The sanctuary was hush. There sat a multitude whose loneliness and depression and inner brokenness was spilling over, even while they were disguised as the best-dressed political, economic, and social elite of Charlotte, North Carolina. Unlike the public poor whose pain and misery is more visible, the pain of the elegant elite is usually hidden behind the veils of power and wealth and human achievement. But we should remember that the pain is no less brutal, no less crippling.

About that time, Carlyle Marney came into the inner sanctum through the dark paneled doors and ascended the altar as only he could, walking slowly, deliberately. The sanctuary fell silent, waiting for that voice that always rumbled like thunder piercing the silence, capturing the ear and the heart and the soul of all who sat motionless—longing for a word.

Marney stood silent. He gazed out on the congregation and finally said, "Sometimes, you study and you long for words to say. You pray and you plead. You beg and you

yearn. You sweat and you struggle, and you come up empty."
Silence. And in the silence, Marney turned and descended the
pulpit and left the sanctuary.

Now, tell me, have you ever wanted to leave the sanctuary
because you had to preach something, when you didn't have
anything to say? Sometimes we cannot speak because we
have not heard and sometimes we cannot speak because the
mystery is too deep for our frail words.

The plague of certainty, this urge to have all the answers,
numbs our souls to the power of mystery and the gift of
silence. But, let us be clear: silence sometimes becomes our
most eloquent testimony.

Ultimately, the wonder of the gospel will not be captured
by wide-screen religious productions or an electrifying drama
about the violent death of Jesus. You and I are not magically
made whole by the tragedy of the crucifixion. It may be good
theater. It is bad theology.

The real wonder of the gospel is the deep, unspeakable,
awesome mystery of God's presence walking here among us,
holding onto us. The gospel is that not even our most hidden
or personal sins, the sins that haunt us in the deep night, can
defeat God's unconditional acceptance of us. God will never
leave our side.

You and I walk among our people as pilgrims of hope.
Our hope, and the hope of those who hover under your wings
of caring, does not rest in knowing enough, but in being
known inside and out and being loved anyhow.

My word is that we should climb our way to the pulpit
each Sunday, and whatever else we have to say, we come
there believing the unspeakable mystery that God loves every
person within the sound of your voice with reckless abandon.

You don't believe it because you know it. You know it because you believe it.

You and I are not bulwarks of certainty. People with all the right answers are dangerous people. They may be clothed as Jewish Zionists. They may be clothed as Christian fundamentalists or Muslim Jihadists. But they are all the same fabric—the fabric of tragedy and evil in the guise of religious devotion.

So, I offer you images for shaping our preaching in an era marked by tragedy, fear, and uncertainty.

The thundering hooves of Esau, deck chairs strewn by the rough seas, silence born of the reality that God is beyond our grasp.

Our calling, my friends, is not to explain the truth. Our calling is to open people's hearts to be embraced by the wonder and the mystery and the transforming power of God's grace.

Grace as a theological concept is trivial and largely inconsequential. But when God's reckless, unconditional acceptance takes hold of us, our preaching, our ministries, and our lives are radically, unspeakably altered.

Beware the plague of certainty. We cannot know enough. We cannot learn enough. We cannot be certain enough to find our way home. Our understanding is flawed. Our words are frail.

We can only rest in the hope that grace, not certainty, will lead us home.

Recentering the Church and Its Ministry

I have learned what it's like to walk up close to the Baptist fires. You and I live in an era that is being defined by religious conflict. The solution to our conflicts will not be in whose religion can be the biggest bully. The truth is that religion in our world is becoming as much a source of tragedy as it is of hope. We are living in a world where religion has become evil and destructive. Christian, Jewish, and Muslim faiths alike have become sources of some of the world's most profound tragedy.

So, let me tell you six trends that I believe will shape the Christian church over the next fifty years.

1. I believe that over the next few decades, fundamentalism will be unmasked and exposed as a fraudulent form of faith. Fundamentalism in all of its expressions worldwide is barbaric and uncivilized, replacing creativity with control and manipulation. It churns out passions that breed religious hatred and bigotry and the twisted wreckage of misplaced devotion. The ascendance of fundamentalist passion and the rhetoric of holy destruction—an oxymoron if I ever heard one—is contributing to the demise of humankind, diminishing our higher calling to love mercy and to do justice, and places the progress of human creation in peril. There is not a dime's worth of difference in Christian, Baptist, Jewish, or Islamic fundamentalism. They are all dangerous, evil forms of religious commitment. People who main and kill and destroy and put other people down in the name of God are children of evil

and the appeal to God's name does not bring sanctity to their work. Holy meanness is still meanness!

Clearly, terrorism spawned by religious fundamentalism has become the greatest threat to civilization in the world today. But we should not deceive ourselves into believing that terrorism is the sole possession of Islam. And, we should not remain silent about the ascendance of fundamentalism in our Baptist ranks. Fundamentalism has corroded the Baptist message. It has undermined the Baptist witness. It has set Baptists, as a denomination, adrift in the sea of insignificance, and fundamentalism will ultimately be exposed as a fraudulent form of faith. In the end it will fail because it is evil.

2. Trend two. There will be increasingly less interest in denominations, and more compelling interest in church engagement. Believe me, people are flocking to churches not because they are caught up with the power and promise of the Cooperative Program. They are not. People climb their way into the sanctuary Sunday after Sunday to try to glimpse enough light and hope to find their way home, to find enough meaning to face the dread and turmoil that consumes them every day. People will increasingly be drawn to churches that capture their hearts and their hands, churches that engage their minds and their talents. We want to belong to a church that will help us become better people and where we might even make the world a little better place.

People come to our places of worship wanting above all else to be set free from the cold and wintry chill of discouragement. They want to warm themselves by the fire of God. Denominations will fade in importance as night follows day because they have become lifeless and abstract. The soothing sounds of serving Jesus too often simply veil the real agenda of control and power. Congregations that are human and personal, congregations making a difference, believing and caring, are the congregations that will have the power to sustain.

3. Trend three. Mark it down. Don't ever forget it. The Church of the twenty-first century will be led more by women, less by men. The twenty-first century will be the century of the woman. For starters, there are more women than men. Not because more women are born, but because girl babies survive better and they live longer. Women are clearly the stronger breed. It has been said that whatever women do, they have to do it twice as well as men to be thought half as good. Fortunately, that's not difficult. But it turns out that women are smarter and better educated than men. Let me be a little more precise. The bell curve for intelligence is tighter for women than for men, which means that there are more geniuses in the world that are men. But, there are a lot more stupid people who are men.

- In 1970, 400,000 businesses were owned by women. Now it's more than ten million.
- In 1970, one percent of business travel was done by women. Now it's fifty percent.
- By 2050, fifty percent of the Fortune 500 will have women CEOs.

Why? Not because of ERA. No. Look at the facts. Boys are four times as likely to drop out of school as girls. More than half of the undergraduate and graduate degrees are going to women. More than half the law students are women. More than half the medical students are women. One-third of our engineers are women, and the number is rising. Talent will prevail.

Now, Baptists had better change their ways because disaster is coming our way. If we think that Baptists can remain a relevant denomination by diminishing the role of women, we are dead wrong. This denomination will rush headlong into a Baptist black hole of irrelevance, unless we change our ways.

4. Trend four. The Christian Church will and must become less exclusive and more relational. Christians must become more open to conversation with other world religions. God not only visits churches. God visits mosques and synagogues. I am working on a new book entitled "Is God a Christian." Baptists and other Christian groups, Presbyterians, Lutherans, and on and on, have turned inward, feuding among themselves and with one another. The feuding is often a way of disguising our sense of futility and the emptiness of our religious devotion. It is a way of trying to prop up a denomination that is growing senile and out of touch with reality. These feuds are sheer nonsense, and childish nonsense at that. Our quarrels are so trivial. In the next fifty years, we must learn to meet at the boundaries of our respective faiths. That's our current challenge. We must be prepared to confess the light by which we live and listen, really listen, to one another and search for our common ground. We must acknowledge that a Jew may have a word from God for us to hear. We must acknowledge that a Muslim may have a word from God for us to hear. Being a faithful Christian is not about the defeat of another person's faith. It is about affirming our faith clearly and openly and leaving every person free to say Yes or No.

5. Trend five. The future of the Church lies with laity, not with the priests. Preachers are not, and never have been, the hope of the world. We at Mercer are in the business of educating clergy because we believe that the clergy play a critically important role in the life and future of the church. But, in the future, we are likely to see more and more

institutes for laity. Among the most important experiences young seminarians have are the internships and mentoring of pastors and congregations. Over and over again these students tell us that they have learned more from the people than from the church staff.

"Preacher-centric" churches rise and fall. They rarely have staying power because they are more show than substance. The years ahead will reward those churches who look to the presence, the power, and the potency of laypeople. As pastors, we need to store it in the recesses of our minds. Laity will fuel the future of the church.

6. Trend six. The recentering of the church will witness the eclipse of entertainment religion. I realize that many of you feel like you have to respond to what the culture requires. I simply urge caution. *Saturday Night Live* Christianity mostly represents the trivialization of belief. The Christian faith is not about making enough noise to drown out the pain. It is about facing pain and finding a glimpse of hope.

The power of worship is being buried beneath the debris of trivial entertainment and "preacher-centric" celebrations. I know, these preacher-centric celebrations feel good, but it is important to resist the transformation of the power of worship into the worship of preaching and preachers.

In our time, the most successful preachers have found their way to stardom. And we gather at the annual Convention meetings to let the stars come out. Stardom is addictive— more addictive than crack cocaine or the heady heights of heroine. The siren call of stardom is more than most of us can withstand. The mirage of adulation and affection, the sustained applause, and the clamoring of folk who just want to touch the hem of your garment are aphrodisiacs too powerful to resist.

There is no drunkenness like the drunkenness of power and acclaim. The mere notion that a star could fall, that the light could go out, is banished from our minds. It is run, rabbit, run. It is burn, baby, burn. It is preach, brother, preach. Pretty soon, an advisory cadre gathers around you to remind you, to reassure you, when you doubt that you are god and to make sure that the mere masses don't actually get too close. The splendor of stardom can hold us in its grasp and we dread the moment that someone turns out the lights.

We need to walk with caution. Rock religion is built on sand. It will not sustain us when we get wounded and crippled or when we are bruised and beaten by the storms that shake our foundations. Write it down. Entertainment religion will fade because down deep it is shallow.

Facing these changes which are hurtling toward us, what must we do, both as churches and ministers, to cope with the church's changing landscape? I offer these modest affirmations that are bubbling within me about directions we must go and lessons we must learn.

1. I believe we must work at recentering and rediscovering the unspeakable mystery of our faith. We have walked so far away from the person we call Jesus. The Christian faith is not about the worship of Jesus. Worshipping Jesus is a dreadful distortion of our faith. The Christian faith is about something far more difficult.

The Christian faith is not about painting "Jesus Saves" on all the rocks in public parks or even about wearing a wristband with "WWJD." It is far easier and it is a lot more popular to worship Jesus, to paint rocks and wear bracelets, than it is to follow Jesus.

Jesus' coming was not about establishing a giant corporate religion called Christianity. Our giant corporate religion will decay. If we want to know what Jesus would do, we must be willing to relate the way Jesus related. We must be prepared to embrace the radical ways that Jesus embodied. Jesus was not even a Christian. He was a Jew from the day he was born until the day he died.

Above all else, the Christian faith is about how we connect, how we meet one another, and how we understand our presence in the world.

There is no magic here, but there is a profound mystery here. Recentering means, again and again, coming to a new way of seeing ourselves and a new way of seeing other people—those we like and those we don't like—a new way of understanding Jesus' presence in the world and a new way of understanding our presence in the world. The power of Christian faith cannot be put into words. Recentering our faith means embracing the mystery. We need to spend more time in silence, more time kneeling, more time caring, more time forgiving.

The Christian faith is not about erecting mountains of doctrine or preserving giant denominational power structures. Our faith is first and foremost about following Jesus. If you want to recenter the church, do not *worship* Jesus. Do something more compelling, more transforming: *follow* Jesus.

2. My second recentering affirmation is this: Grace is life's most important gift. The stunning news that brings people hope is not the admonition that they have got to believe in God. That's not good news. That's scary news because sometimes I wonder if God is really there. Our faith has better news than that. The really good news is not that we believe in God but that God believes in us. God is with us. God is in us, and God is for us. God lives on our street, eats at our table, sleeps in our bed, walks on our treadmill, sits at our desk, and listens to our music.

If the church is to flourish, we cannot build our religious lives around a gospel of fear, or a gospel of reward for our meanness. The Christian faith is not about being afraid of God. Fear may get us to submit, but fear always leads to anger and resentment and bitterness.

We must learn that grace is life's most important gift. Above all else, the church must become a reservoir of grace.

3. A third affirmation and, indeed, I believe a lesson we must learn. We should tuck it away deep within our inner souls and when everything grows quiet and the light dims, listen to its sound.

The word is this: the ultimate measure of our lives, for clergy and laity alike, will not be how much we have gained, but how much we have given. The measure will not be how far we have run or how high we have climbed, not how many sermons we have preached or even how long we have lived. The ultimate measure will be how deeply we have loved.

Most of you know that as a college president, I raise money for a living. I love to ask people for money. On one occasion about two years ago, I was visiting a gentleman in Florida. I asked him for two million dollars. He agreed to that gift, and after some conversation, we decided to have lunch together. While we were having lunch, I began to tell him that in all my years of raising money for the University, I had discovered that people who are able to give are generally healthier and happier people than those who could not bring themselves to give. Some folk are so possessed by their possessions that they clutch them ever so tightly, as if they were holding on to life itself. We had a great conversation, and I left and returned to Macon.

About two weeks later, I was sitting in my office, and my Jacksonville friend called me on the phone and said, "Kirby, will you tell me again how good I am supposed to feel." I said, "Bill, if you don't feel good, you haven't given enough. I don't want you to give until it hurts. I want you to give until it feels good." The ultimate measure of our lives will not be how much we have gained, but how much we have given.

4. My fourth and final recentering affirmation has to do with those of you who have found the courage to walk with the mantle of ministry. It can be a heavy mantle. I am a "preacher watcher." I am very interested in the perils of preaching and I believe that you and I must continually revisit the power and meaning of being the priests of God. Yogi Berra said, "You can observe a lot just by watching." So, I will conclude my reflections about where we go from here with three observations for recentering our ministry.

1. The work of the church on this changing landscape and the capacity of the ministry to shepherd our congregations of faith are being crippled by wounded priests who have nowhere to turn. Countless people who nobly call themselves the priests of God are trapped in a cauldron of isolation, loneliness, fear, and doubt. I am not speaking here of the publicized pedophiles and the tragic misfortunes that have been created by the misguided commitment to celibacy with the Roman Catholic Church. I am speaking of wounds that are far closer. Right here where we are and among hundreds of our colleagues, ministers are quietly, silently, tragically bearing wounds, wounds that they cannot let go. They are putting on faces of caring while being devoured by inner pain and isolated with the sense that no one cares. We are too often priests who have no priests. Without a place and a relationship of refuge, our courage will inevitably turn to despair. If you are to be a priest, you must find a priest.

2. My second affirmation for those who wear the mantle of ministry is rule number 5 of the Kansas General Assembly,

an immutable law discovered by my friend and colleague, Robert L. Steed. It came out of the nineteenth century and is a simple, but profound philosophical principle. Actually, the first four rules have been lost in history. Only rule 5 remains. This simple gift of philosophical wisdom goes like this: "Don't take yourself so damn serious."

In our world, people often treat ministers and college presidents with respect, even a certain deference. That's not a bad thing, but ever believing it is a bad thing. The first thing you know, we begin to walk with a hint of arrogance and speak with a note of condescension and authority. It is all a tragic mistake. The truth is that we don't know more than anybody else. We are not smarter or wiser. The first sign of real wisdom is to take ourselves lightly, to confess our own humanness. Because sometimes we don't know what to say. We don't know what to do. About the best we can do is just to be there with our uncertainty showing, caught somewhere between halting words and speechless silence. It is, after all, frail humans who put on the mantle of ministry. Learn to laugh at your own frailties. Remember rule number 5. "Don't take yourself so damn serious."

3. My third recentering word for those who have the courage to preach is to discover that the power of preaching does not reside in speaking. the power of preaching resides in listening and learning. Your sheer status as pastor, as church leader, may determine who speaks. But your capacity to keep learning will determine who listens.

We listen in many ways. We listen by reading. We listen with our ears. We listen with our eyes, we listen with our silence. Examine your listening quotient. Let me be very practical. The right ratio is about five to one. Spend eighty percent of your time listening—listening with your ears, listening with your eyes, listening with your hearts, listening with your silence. Spend twenty percent of your time speaking. The more inverted your quotient becomes, the less you will have to say and the more irrelevant your voice will become.

When speaking to corporate leaders, I often remind them that "the person who is silent is in control of the conversation." The effectiveness of your ministry is likely to be shaped more by the quality of your listening than the quality of your preaching. Listening and learning will stretch your capacity to lead.

The changing landscape of the church will require that we recenter the church and its ministry. We should not become trapped by the way things have been. Our challenge is to find the courage to listen again for God's voice. God's voice may come to us from unexpected quarters. Our challenge as a church is to transform ourselves into congregations of light and hope in a world where religious delusion has become a part of the human problem. Our challenge will be whether this century we have just entered will turn out to be a march toward religious desolation and the irrelevance of the Christian Church, or whether we will find the courage to recalibrate our vision, to recenter our faith and our ministry. Our challenge is to walk beyond the wilderness of religion run amuck toward a faith that can lead us to the promised land of light and hope.

The Baptist Journey of Faith and Learning[*]

I am a Baptist. My vocation is education. And my vocation has allowed me to bring together my life of learning and my life of faith.

Neither journey has been without its troubles and its turmoil. They never are.

In my journeys within education I have seen Baptist schools and secular universities up close. And I have been part of a Baptist university as it has struggled to shape its character. I have weighed in on the side of making Mercer a Baptist university. But the struggle is never-ending.

My journey of faith has carried me through the dead heat of Baptist turmoil. I have mourned our losses and been preoccupied with our defeats. But I see a new day coming.

I am learning that being Baptist is a much larger world, a much higher calling than being just a *Southern* Baptist. My journey has taken me beyond the boundaries of Southern Baptists. But I have no quarrel with Southern Baptists. I have no quarrel with those brothers and sisters who need to hold onto the mantle of being a Southern Baptist. It is their comfort zone. But out of the mourning called grief, I have come to the

---

[*]An earlier version of this address appeared in *Christian Ethics Today: Journal of Christian Ethics* 5 (March 1996) ©The Christian Ethics Today Foundation, and may be accessed online at <http://www.christianethicstoday.com/Issue/005/The%20Baptist%lo20 Journey%20of%20Faith%20and%20Learning%20by%20R.%20 Kirby%20Godsey_005__.htm>.

dawning of a new morning called light. For me, being Baptist is a higher calling.

Southern Baptists continue to be a large denomination. They continue to be powerful. They continue to be rich. They have achieved giant corporate status and they wield real political clout. But in the process, they seem to have buried much of the treasure of being Baptist.

We have witnessed, firsthand, a religious debacle—one more denomination suffering from decay, losing its soul in search of political power and religious prestige.

But it would be self-centered to lose heart. Baptists are not, after all, the hope of the world. God's world is not somehow waiting silently to see what in the world happens to Baptists. To think that the hope of humankind depends upon politics in Nashville is myopic and arrogant. Baptists have never been the source of all truth and we have not become the center of God's universe.

Our only reason for being has been to serve as instruments of hope and grace. More simply put, Baptist were not called to become one more corporate giant in neon lights. Baptists were called to be simple priests, bearers of light, a family of faith living out the reality of God's presence in our world.

We do the best we can but when it comes to religious organizations, we can usually recognize the signs of decay. We become rigid and exclusive, confident that we have a corner on God's truth. We become preoccupied with the contours of the denomination. We reorganize and streamline. We begin to quarrel over the boundaries—whether here or there, a little to the left or a little to the right.

We should have seen it coming. We began to look to our feuds and to our close votes to add excitement and stamina to our meetings. We began to squabble about who had the truth and whose truth and message would prevail. It was mostly nonsense. Surely we do not believe that God is really interested in our petty disputes.

My celebration of being Baptist has brought me to the Cooperative Baptist Fellowship. For me, the CBF was born, not to lick our wounds, not to weep together in our defeat, not to compete against the jubilant noise of those who have taken over the SBC. The CBF was born as a way of recentering ourselves on the truth that

- We are not here to fight. We are here to minister.
- We are not here to shout or demean one another. We are here to preach and to teach.
- We are not here to recite the right religious ideology. We are here to forgive.
- We are not here to eclipse the gospel with our mindless bickering. We are here to embody the gospel in our own honest caring.
- We are not enforcers. We are not the Gestapo for some misguided form of Calvinism. You and I are here to give flesh and blood to the gospel.
- We are not here to make sure that people recite the right language. We are here to be God's people.
- We are not here to require that people embrace the latest version of fundamentalist orthodoxy. We are here to give people hope, to bear light amidst the shadows, to teach, to live out grace. We are here to help people in Jesus' name and to ask questions later.

Caring is not something grandiose. It is not a theological proposition. It is certainly not a denominational posture. Caring is not a skyscraper. It is not a new organizational structure. Caring is not about getting a patent on the name of Lottie Moon.

Caring means to heal the sick, to help the poor, to shelter the homeless, to teach the ignorant. It means setting people free of disease and setting them free of prejudice. It means looking out for people who are lonely and taking up for people who are powerless.

The fact is that Southern Baptists have become like most other denominational organizations, less Baptist and more authoritarian, less grace and more hype. Over and over again, churches and denominations become servants of the culture. Power and popularity. The rhythms of Saturday night become the beat of Sunday morning. Jesus slips out the back door unnoticed to go look after the hungry.

My journey teaches me that as Baptists grow and succeed, they inevitably become enamored with their own success. The first thing you know we find ourselves trying to manipulate denominational politics—fundamentalists and moderates alike, while the homeless are sleeping under bridges and violence and abuse run rampant in our streets.

Being Baptist is a higher calling. Being Baptist is about caring, and caring is a different calling. It is God's call. It means bringing water to the thirsty in Jesus' name, pushing back the shadows of ignorance in Jesus' name. So being Baptist calls us back to our beginnings. Our birthright lies in lifting people up in Jesus' name. And unless helping people in Jesus' name prevails, our rhetoric and our proclamations and our political convocations—called Baptist "conventions"—are nothing more than a noisy charade that veils the skeletal remains of a dead denomination.

None of us is exempt from the perils of success. The Cooperative Baptist Fellowship will have to struggle to hold onto its soul. We do not gather in the Fellowship to be one more political forum.

- We gather to celebrate our faith as Baptists—a people who are free to believe, free to listen out for God, free to respond to God's call unencumbered by race or gender or political persuasion.
- We gather as people who are free to worship and free to think, free to hold Jesus high as the Word of God and free to interpret the Bible as the record of God's revelation.
- We gather as people who are free to be the church, free to preach, and free to teach.

The formation of the CBF should give us courage to be Baptists again, to loose ourselves from the bitterness and the fear and the resentment of being part of a denomination that has wasted much of its passion and energy in the raging war of power politics. Let us never be drawn back into that *un*civil war. If the fundamentalists win or the liberals win, Baptists lose. Among Southern Baptists, the fundamentalists won. Baptists lost.

My Baptist journey has also carried me to the towers of academe. Success in academia is just as enchanting as success in the denomination. I watched and listened as colleagues would have Mercer to be done with our Baptist connections. Shake the Baptist dust from our feet. It is an enchanting idea. It has been a road I have chosen not to take. As a Baptist university, I believe we must be a force for preserving our Baptist identity and our Baptist principles.

When I study Baptist history, I am astonished by the historical significance of education in the rise of the missionary impulse.

The missionary force in the early nineteenth century was awash on the shoals of Baptist conflict. Almost dead. Opposition to missions was fierce. Some associations in

Georgia struggled against the notion of a Baptist general convention precisely because it would encourage missions and education.

At the September 1822 meeting of the Hephzibah Baptist Association, a motion to join the new General Baptist Association of Georgia in extending the gospel "by missions and missionaries" was met with this response: A motion was made to lay the matter on the table, amended by a motion to throw the matter *under* the table, and then by another, to kick the bearer of the motion out of the house. This motion was carried by a rising vote, some members leaping up and down to emphasize their vote and afterwards escorting the motion-maker out the door, threatening physical harm if he ever again pronounced the word "missions" in the presence of that body.

Study Baptist history and you will discover that it was in the formation of a commitment to Christian education that the antimissionary spirit was overcome. We have largely lost our connection to those roots. In so doing, we have lost our bearings. And what has become of us? In a work that began together, a great divide has emerged between missions and education, with enormous tension between the priests and scribes. But unless the preachers and the teachers, the priests and the scribes, the men and women of letters, and the men and women of the spirit can sit down together, our cooperative efforts, whether in a convention or a fellowship, will flounder in a sea of pettiness and triviality. Evangelism that is content to paint "Jesus Saves" on all the rocks in public parks will fail. Education that presumes to separate the mind from the spirit will fail. Witness that is uninformed and uncaring will fail.

Missions and evangelism desperately need the resources of education, and education desperately needs the power and the presence of honest faith. My journey has taught me that while churches and denominations may speak of Christian education, their real passion is for college football. But being Baptist has taught me that we cannot separate missions and education. We cannot separate thinking and believing.

Just as a denomination can lose the soul of being Baptist, a Baptist college or university or seminary can surely abandon their Baptist heritage. For our Baptist schools, it has been a double siege, a double-edged sword. There is the siege of those without who want to control our schools, to mandate our textbooks, to prescribe creeds to which teachers must give assent. There is the siege of those within who wish to abort any identity with the church.

On both fronts, we cannot be a good Baptist university, a good Baptist college, or a good Baptist seminary if either siege prevails. Within our institutions, we must bear witness to our faith and make clear to our students that the real trouble of our world is not that people don't know enough. It is that they are not good enough.

From without, we must overcome the fear of open inquiry and intellectual freedom. The mind and the spirit are not in conflict. We need not be defensive. God needs no defense and truth will be its own protection.

Now permit me a final word about my journey. For me, being a Baptist by faith and an educator by vocation, converges in Mercer's decision to undertake theological education. My journey of faith and my journey of learning have come together as we join hands with Baptists to create the McAfee School of Theology.

At Mercer, our journey has brought us here because it is where we began in 1833. Jesse Mercer established Mercer University in order to influence and to foster "pious intelligence," a phrase used by Elder Mercer in his draft of the Constitution of the General Association of Georgia Baptists at Powelton in 1822. So, Jesse Mercer's lamp, Jesse Mercer's vision, has become a light for our path.

Piety means knowing that you cannot understand your life and I cannot understand my life without reference to God. Piety means finding life's center. Piety is not sentimental or foolish. It is not about public prayer or giving out tracts. Piety is about finding a guiding light for our path. Piety means finding the purity of heart to will one thing. You and I are many people. We are distracted and scattered among many allegiances. Piety means finding a center for devotion that can bring order and meaning out of the chaos of our lives.

Yet, piety alone is not enough. A School of Theology should bring piety and thought together. The mind is a gift of God. Any notion that being devout means to turn away from thought is a caricature of truth and holiness. Speaking without thought leads to arrogant ignorance. Arrogance and ignorance are a lethal combination. It will numb the mind and kill the spirit.

So I say, let us never fear the search for truth. Let the teachers teach and let the preachers preach. God's truth will prevail.

Education that is controlled and limited by creedal boundaries is not education at all. Education that has been purified in the sieve of doctrinaire orthodoxy is not education at all. It is not even good training. We want to build a school where people can teach without fear of doctrinal listeners outside the door and where students can study without fear of intimidation and religious demagoguery.

Mercer University began a School of Theology for four reasons.

1. We believe that the demise and takeover of the Baptist seminaries by the denominational mafia is a moral outrage.

2. We believe that theological education must be free and open, intellectually honest and faithful, or it is not worthy to be called education at all.
3. We have listened to Baptists. Mercer University was founded by Baptists, nurtured by Baptists, and we must serve Baptists.
4. We have a new vision of theological education. We have established this school, not to replicate Southern Seminary or Southeastern Seminary, but here among the heart of Baptists, to create and to sustain a new vision for theological education.

Ours is a vision that reaches across the boundaries of thought and experience of clergy and laity. We will seek to educate men and women who can serve our churches with the passion of faith and the integrity of thought. We are aiming to bring up a new generation of pastors and church leaders who love the church, who understand the Bible, and who are devoted followers of Jesus Christ.

One final lesson I have learned from my Baptist journey is that we do not go alone. The best evidence that God is with us is that we hold on to one another.

I believe that if we hold onto one another, God will be with us and we will find our way to the Promised Land. There will be twists and turns. There will be sharp curves and steep hills. We will stumble and someone will have to pick us up and brush us off. But if we walk together and follow God's light, we will find the Promised Land where faith and learning can stand together. And we will be Baptists, not because we believe the same doctrine, but because we serve the same Lord.

Pious Intelligence:
The Challenge of Christian Education

Many of us involved in the independent sector of higher education have come to our places on pathways that are closely associated with a very specific religious tradition. Religious affirmation is a vital part of the history of many of our educational institutions, and, equally so, our own institutional histories have significantly influenced the development of our religious and church constituencies.

But, I come today not to speak of our past but to speak of the challenges that face us in the future and to suggest that addressing those challenges will require us to take more seriously the spiritual dimensions of our histories. In the university where I serve, the relationship to its Baptist heritage should not, in my view, be seen simply as a memorial to the past. Quite frankly, that perspective has been the course of action chosen by many of our own church-related colleges and universities. It is my conviction that these historical relationships can hold the promise of the future.

My theme is that the prospects for a vital future spring from taking hold of the vision that created our beginnings. Institutions cannot be nourished through abstract images of themselves. Our institutions, and those of us who lead them, must be captured by a concrete notion of why we are here.

Some years ago while rummaging through the history of Georgia Baptists, I came upon this statement, which I have chosen to make the focus of these remarks. More than a century and a half ago, those persons who were committed to

Christian education in our own religious context defined the
first purpose of their association in these words:

1. To unite the influence and *pious intelligence* of
   Georgia Baptists, and thereby facilitate their union
   and cooperation.*

"Pious intelligence." It is an unusual, perhaps archaic jux-
taposition of words. Piety today runs away from being too
closely associated with intellectualism, and the pursuit of
intelligence is prepared to lay aside any devotion to piety. I
believe that the future of our schools, if we have a serious
commitment to Christian education, must be built around an
uncompromising commitment to "pious intelligence." The
two belong together. We are foolish if we think we can build
outstanding private universities who have their grounding in
religious affirmation or piety alone. The future of our schools
must be built upon intelligence as well. We must lay claim to
intelligence as a gift of God.

We need to speak plainly. The prospects for any great
institution or great religious denomination cannot ignore the
power of the mind without being dominated by a world of
sheer fantasy. Piety that cannot bear the counsel of the mind
is no piety at all, but an eclipse of real discipleship. If we are
to meet the challenges of Christian education, we must be
prepared to declare the meaning of piety and to lay claim to
the importance of intelligence. We must bring together both
piety and thought.

----

*From article 10 of the constitution of the General Association
of Georgia Baptists (1822), drafted by Jesse Mercer. Italics added.

First, this matter of intelligence. The best future for our society, indeed, the human order, does not rest in the preservation of isolated and random brilliance but in the encouragement and the nurturing of intelligence. Intelligence expresses itself most fundamentally in the willingness to reflect, to think before we act, and to suspend quick and easy judgments in favor of reasoned reflection.

Intelligence. Our personal histories rely upon it. The future of our religious orders will rely upon it. The future of our nation will be imperiled without it. It is often easier to follow the herd mentality and to become victimized by the emotional outbursts of people who are around us. Our likes and dislikes, what we value and what we reject, come to be determined by the mood and the will of people with whom we live. You and I live in clusters, in towns and communities, in sectors and suburbs, in ghettos and metroplexes. Part of the reason we live there is so that we will not have to think. We can watch one another, follow one another, hold on to one another, and abandon any responsibility for deciding and acting.

The purpose of education in the future should be found in giving us the strength to do otherwise. It means to harness the power of intelligence for our lives and to recover the power of the mind. It means to learn to make intelligent decisions, to make independent and informed judgments. It means to relate to one another as thoughtful persons whose need is not to control but to respect.

Ignorance causes us to chatter at one another when we have nothing to say. Intelligence causes us to be quiet.

Ignorance causes us to shout when we doubt. Intelligence causes us to listen.

Ignorance causes us to be demagogues, imposing our religious and political views on other people. Intelligence causes us to temper our passions with reason and tolerance.

Ignorance is causing many of our religious groups to turn on themselves and to destroy themselves with self-interested despotism. Indeed, if there is anything worse than political demagoguery, it is probably religious demagoguery. Each form calls upon us to dismantle our intelligence in favor of the idolatry of narrow-minded littleness. If we are able to resist demagoguery wherever it occurs—in our institutions, in the church, in the society, in the State Houses—our most significant resource will be the nurturing of intelligence. It means having people who are capable of thinking for themselves. If our religious commitments cannot withstand people thinking for themselves, those commitments face an uneasy future.

The destinies of our schools should honor the power of intelligence. Intelligence affects everything we are and everything we do.

It affects whether we treat each other with dignity and respect or with condescension and prejudice.

It affects whether we approach our work with responsibility and discipline or with shabby performance and inferior expectations.

It affects whether our nation will pursue endless nuclear annihilation or whether it will prefer the course of dialogue and open debate.

It affects whether a religious denomination will sacrifice its own destiny on the anvil of petty disputes or place religious openness before theological agreement.

It affects whether we educate people to recite easy answers or to wrestle with difficult problems.

The future of our schools, if they are to be the centers of academic strength for which we long, lives in the vision of our forebearers. They must become places of learning that hold high the place of reason, knowing that reason is not the enemy of God.

We should not be afraid to pursue the course of truth. Intelligence looks to the honest and candid pursuit of truth in the confidence that God stands behind our search. Our schools should never seek to protect people from the canons of truth. If our pursuit of learning contradicts our view of God, it may be that God is trying to tell us something.

Too long we have sanctified our ignorance and intellectual laziness with our affirmations of faith. God's truth and the ultimate reality of the universe are the same and the objective pursuit of knowledge and the intimate reverence for God will never lead us to different places. The future of our world needs those persons who can think critically and who can choose wisely. It will honor those persons who can see with insight, who can speak with conviction, who can make principled judgments in the midst of confusion and conflict. The future will honor the power and the presence of intelligence.

Intelligence, however, is not enough. Francis Bacon said that "knowledge is power." But education is not enough. The future of our centers of learning should be built upon bringing piety and thought together. We must encourage and be willing to place the weight of our own administrative influence behind "pious intelligence." It is a splendid phrase, rich with meaning and insight.

We have populations exploding and people dying of starvation only one thousand miles away in Mexico. It is a time bomb. We need pious intelligence.

We have nuclear warheads aimed nervously at one another in the worried hope that no terrorist will figure out the combinations that will launch our arsenals. We need pious intelligence.

We have Third World nations, through the wonder of radio and television, watching in their villages, angry that our achievements and our opulence are not lifting them out of the mud. We need pious intelligence.

There is no guarantee that the human race as we know it is here to stay. We may end up killing one another and leaving this little minor Planet Earth as one more silent rock in the wilderness of space, while God starts over somewhere else. We need pious intelligence.

Our society is one that has come to honor neutral intelligence. Education has become largely an affair of the state where we are to teach and to learn devoid of spiritual bearings or ultimate meanings. In 1860, there were approximately 150 institutions of higher learning in this country. Less than ten percent of those institutions were related primarily to the state. Quite to the contrary, in that time education was first and foremost moral education where students were brought to struggle with the ultimate issues of right and wrong and good and evil.

The highest future of our colleges and universities will, in my judgment, be centered on the pursuit of pious intelligence. We have somehow allowed the notion of piety to be identified with superficiality and sentimental religious devotion. It is a mistake. By pious, I mean to signal an understanding of the reverence for life, to see that a person's life, indeed the meaning of the world itself, cannot be fathomed without reference to God. I mean through the meaning of pious to convey the power of the spiritual dimensions of our existence. You and I are what we care about. We are what we value. We are what we believe is ultimately important. We are who we love and we are what we choose to believe in.

The problems of humankind cannot be resolved with pure intelligence and this is the heart of my comments. The issues facing us will not be solved only by whether we know enough. The issues can be solved only if we are good enough. The future of our civilization will require that intelligence be combined with sensitivity and compassion. We must be able to make commitments that are trustworthy. We must be able to speak with honesty and integrity.

Sensitivity, compassion, commitment, honesty, and integrity. These are the qualities of being together that will transform intelligence into pious intelligence. It is not that we need to merely think more clearly but we also need to care about one another more deeply. Wisdom will spring from the integration of thought and reverence. If we cannot get beyond our own self-interest, our self-interest itself will be victimized by the lack of thoughtful reverence.

I am suggesting that the future of our schools should be built upon taking seriously the ultimate bearings of our lives. We must build places of learning that are committed to helping people not only to think clearly but also to act with grace and integrity.

Several signposts will keep us on the track of integrating piety and thought. I will mention three here.

In the first place, our educational endeavors must hold on to open and honest inquiry. The traditional liberal arts will be a resource to us in this respect. In our need to acquire students and the constant pressure to make our programs vocationally relevant, we should lay claim to "classical and literary" learning as a powerful integrating force of the human spirit. The world of practical learning will become desolate without the values reflected in classical learning.

What are those values? Analysis, criticism, openness, the tolerance of dissent, cultural transcendence. We need to challenge those who study with us to become friends with the great writers, to be critical analysts so that we are less immobilized by rhetoric and the passion of the moment. We need to learn to communicate ideas crisply with precision and clarity. Our schools, in spite of their diversity and professionalism, have the center of their being rooted in critical and thoughtful reflection. Take away the commitment to careful thinking, precise analysis, and principled judgment, and our schools and colleges will become merely a collection of disparate, dangling subjects. Without intelligence, anarchy will prevail.

One sign of pious intelligence will be institutions who are able to maintain open inquiry and critical analysis, as well as assure that the traditional liberating arts remain a central component of our commitment to teaching and learning.

Another signpost along the way is whether we are willing to learn that worship is a part of learning. Worship is more listening than speaking. It is more silence than proclamation. Pious intelligence means deliberately opening ourselves to the divine perspective coming to bear on our human experience. It means waiting before God and before one another for understanding and insight.

The tragedy of religion today is not that we believe too little. It is that we believe too much. Our devotion is scattered. We chase after the chilling uniformity of religious orthodoxy. It is not important that the students in our colleges and universities leave these places of learning with a neat package of religious answers. Pious intelligence rarely proposes a basket of answers. It is more likely to offer five loaves and two fishes of intellectual understanding and an open affirmation of religious commitment, and then tell us to go feed the hungry multitudes.

I call you to a third signpost. Pious intelligence will take us down the road to explore the moral alternatives of human experience. The moral dimension of intelligence means this: Each of us stands in human history as a unique and irrevocable person. No one can be who you are, can think your thoughts, can hear your sounds, or dream your dreams. Moral education means having the will to face our own peculiar destiny and to fulfill in history our own very special reason for being here.

Intelligence may call upon us to live more efficiently. Pious intelligence will call upon us to live more profoundly, to probe the mystery of our own presence in the universe and to bring to bear on our own relationships and our own decisions the moral responsibility of being a child of God.

Pious intelligence. It is incumbent upon us to bring together superior educational possibilities with a confessed religious perspective.

In his 1948 Armistice Day speech, Omar Bradley observed that

> We have grasped the mystery of the atom and rejected the Sermon on the Mount. The world has achieved brilliance without wisdom, power without conscience. Our knowledge of science has outstripped our power to control that knowledge. Ours is a world of nuclear giants and ethical infants. We know more about war than we know about peace, more about killing than we know about living.

Intelligence is not enough.

We need not be defensive. We are not called upon to defend God or to protect the truth. God needs no defense and truth will be its own protector. We are called upon rather to live by the truth, to live as persons freed from the tyranny of our own educational culture. In the process, we will no doubt make some mistakes. But let us not measure either our lives or our institutions by our mistakes. Rather we should measure our lives by our vision, by the breadth of our spirit, by the worth of our commitment.

We should take upon ourselves the responsibility of educating young men and women for every arena of life—to be teachers, to be businessmen, to be lawyers, to be engineers, to be doctors. But we need a new vision of the pressing need for businessmen, for teachers, for lawyers who will bring awareness of the moral dimension to every aspect of their life and work. We can do so only if we believe that human life and human work and human interaction are moral under-takings and that we must address the moral alternatives of human experience as a fundamental part of our mission in higher education.

Pious intelligence means that it is time for us to begin to act from a confessed theological base. We work alongside others who educate and we affirm the good that is accom-plished in institutions outside the arena of Christian edu-cation. The fact is that Christian education can never carry the educational burden of our land. It is imperative, however, that we make our presence felt. The goal of higher education in general is to achieve knowledge. The goal of Christian higher education is to achieve relationships that bear the reality and presence of God's spirit. It is to make God's grace present in the deepest pursuit of learning. Christian education then is built on a different foundation and we will do well to remain in touch with our theological and our spiritual bearings.

Our colleges and universities need from you and me a clear and open commitment to pious intelligence. We need to join hands in shaping educational institutions of the highest caliber. We must measure ourselves by rigorous criteria. In a world that is symbolized by pavements, computers, and shopping centers, we need to offer the human spirit room to breathe, a place to reflect, and a time to see how learning bears on life.

It would be a happy circumstance if the problems of human experience would come to us in the packages of chemistry and biology and history and psychology. But the issues of human life are rarely so clear-cut. Life often hurts, and where learning meets life, we need not only knowledge, we need grace and understanding.

Pious intelligence. Let us learn from our heritage. My word to you is that we should educate openly with a special purpose. If we are willing to lay claim to it, a new spirit of expectation can be born among us and in our institutions. The strength of that spirit will be measured largely by our confidence and our voices as leaders of these institutions. If we are willing to stand and to speak not for piety alone nor for intelligence alone, but for pious intelligence, we can make ourselves a force for insuring that the men and women of the future will be men and women for whom the spirit of learning has not outstripped learning of the spirit.

It will not happen unless you and I are prepared to take a stand. As for me, I will stake my own life and work on this issue: Our highest good lies in bringing together genuine academic excellence with a profound sense of devotion.

I commend to you pious intelligence.

Seeing Our Blindness

Luke, the Jesus storyteller, captures our imagination with the story of St. Paul. It is the story of a man who becomes blind in order to see. Paul's story is remarkably like our own. We, like Paul, are not blinded by the darkness. We are not blinded by evil. We are blinded by our own convictions, blinded by our devotion to do things our way.

Paul was blind before he lost his sight. The most terrible blindness that gripped Paul was not the three days without eyesight. Those days were to be overcome. Paul had become blinded by his passion, crippled by his own certainty—a far more difficult blindness to heal.

Paul was a man on a mission. He was possessed, consumed. His heart and soul were wrapped up in saving his church. His church, strong and established, upright and respected, was being challenged by a young brand of "ne'er do wells." This young gang of Jesus followers were creating doubts among the faithful. It was Paul to the rescue. The church had to be defended.

With relentless conviction, Paul began to go from village to village to round up these unorthodox believers. Before they grew and persuaded others, they had to be snuffed out.

After all, the truth had been delivered to the prophets. The Torah—what we call the Bible—already revealed God's will. This "new gospel" of God's unconditional grace seemed absurd. They feared that if people really believed that God loved them whether they went to church or not, that they would stop going to the synagogue and, even worse, stop giving. It could cause the ecclesiastical house to crumble.

This naïve gospel of Jesus seemed to let people off the hook. It described the ruling preachers of the church as vipers. Paul, a devout follower of Jewish doctrine, was rushing to the rescue of a world of religion being turned upside down.

Along the way of doing the holy work of purging the church of renegades, Paul was blinded by the light. The light of truth always hurts our eyes. The light stopped Paul dead in his tracks. Suddenly and dramatically, he was aware of being blind. Three days of startling blindness became Paul's bridge to being able to see. Neither Paul nor you or I will be able to see until we first face into our blindness.

The Christian faith, if it is faith at all, changes, it irrevocably changes how we see the world. Faith uncovers our blindness. We see a new creation.

The miracle of faith, the only important miracle of faith, is to open our eyes. We see our world, we see ourselves, in a different way.

Frankly, we, like Paul, prefer them closed. The light of God's presence hurts our eyes. We drift back into the shadows. Life feels better there. Blindness chosen is far more devastating and difficult to dispel than blindness given.

People for whom blindness is a physical trauma reach for the power to overcome. They find ways to compensate for that trauma. Those of us for whom blindness is chosen dread the prospect of giving up our blindness. Life in the shadows is pretty good. No sharp distinctions between right and wrong. Our blindness comforts us. We live in the shadows not because the truth is not shining bright but because we like life better there. We want friends and a church that will confirm our prejudices. We prefer religion that doesn't challenge us or confuse us.

So, if we want to step toward a new beginning we must be willing to ask some hard questions.

First, why is our blindness so hard to see?

Second, what peculiar blindness blocks the light of the gospel in our life?

And third, how can we open our eyes?

First, "Why is our blindness so hard to see?" Let us hear this word. The blindness to truth first and foremost occurs because we do not want to see.

Paul did not want to hear the gospel because he had a clear and accepted creed to live by. He had a religion that worked. He went to the temple, studied the law, read the Bible, and recited the prayers of the church. He tithed his earnings. He was a man of faith, a holy man of the church.

He could not see because he already saw God clearly.

Like Paul, we cannot see God because we are possessed by the gods of our own creation. The greatest deterrent to seeing God and hearing God are not the distractions of Satan. It is the siren call of our own gods. We have this god who is a big eye in the sky, shaking his finger at us, saying, "You better be good or else God is going to get you." We create these little gods that in our imagination behave like we would behave if we were God. We cannot see because we are too busy making a god in our image, shaping and polishing our own golden calves.

There is more. We do not see because we like what we see already. Our eyes are full of delight. What we are already seeing is "good looking." We prefer the suburbs to the slums. We prefer the "in crowd" to the "out crowd." We like to look at people and places that are good looking.

Jesus, on the other hand, kept finding himself among the people who were not good looking—the poor, the broken, the bedeviled, the blind. They were people who could not do anything for him. Mother Teresa made trips to New York, to the halls of Congress and the high places of premiers and popes. Beautiful places and beautiful people. But she was consumed by the real world she saw on the back streets of Calcutta.

The truth is that the beautiful blinds us to the ugly. We choose blindness because it looks so good.

Our second question is more difficult: "What peculiar blindness is blocking the gospel in our life?"

Blindness is always very specific. The specific blindness for Paul is unlikely to be our own blindness. We can see his blindness. It is ours that we cannot see. No one here has set out to mount the holocaust that Paul had set out to unleash. We create holocausts of our own. We become victims of our own fantasies. We are blinded by our own prejudices.

In the early 1800s, most people, that is, most "good" people, not the outcasts, the best church people, could not see the blindness of slavery. Preachers were the most outspoken defenders of slavery, citing loud lessons of Holy Scripture. The moral rebellion against slavery was not led by the church. The church was too busy with the justifying of slavery. We called the abolitionists rabble-rousers, instruments of the devil.

Blindness is never easy to see. We can see their blindness. It is ours that we cannot see. We go to great lengths to put God's stamp of approval on our sins.

Blindness sometimes wears the mantle of religion. People kill and maim in the name of God. It is sin. The Reformation occurred because of the excesses and evils of religion. The achievements of the Reformation have largely been lost.

Today, in the world of religion, we worship the practice of worship. It is blindness. We argue about the Bible as if we are protecting God. It is blindness. We claim the Bible to be infallible and inerrant. It is blindness. We worship human doctrine while God requires no allegiance to doctrine. It is blindness.

The Christian faith is not about worshipping worship or paying homage to the Bible or reciting sound doctrine. It is blindness upon blindness. The Christian faith calls us toward a way that is far more simple and profound and transforming. Like Peter and James and John and Paul, our call, yours and mine, is to follow Jesus. Following Jesus will open our eyes to the tragedy and hurt in the world.

The world in which you and I probably live needs less religion and more piety. We praise God most clearly not with jingles about Jesus. We see God more clearly when we act toward one another with integrity, when we treat life as a holy trust.

Blindness haunts us in ways that belong peculiarly to our time. It is easy enough now to recognize the blindness of slavery or segregation or apartheid. It is more difficult, more confusing to see our present blindness, a blindness that generates hatred and meanness, for example, toward gays and lesbians. It is a subject that makes us very uneasy. Methodists and Presbyterians and Baptists vote on what to do with churches that accept gays.

While there may be real debate about the moral status of homosexuality, there should be no debate that being mean and hateful is wrong.

In the next 100 years, we will be able to *engineer* the genetics of your grandchildren's children. It will create new risks of blindness and the world needs, desperately needs, the moral voice of the church.

But let me ask an even more compelling question. What can open our eyes? Does the church contribute to blindness or can the church become a beacon of moral light?

Hear the word of the gospel. We are called to worship the Lord our God with all our mind, with all of our heart, and with all our soul.

Opening our eyes is a long journey. It is a journey we may not want to make. Opening our eyes requires courage—the courage to open our minds, the courage to open our hearts, and the courage to open our spirits. It is not a journey for the fainthearted.

First, if we want to open our eyes, we have to be willing to open our minds. Paul's mind was made up. He knew right from wrong. He knew his way around the synagogue. If our eyes are to be opened we must be willing to learn again. Closed minds generate blind eyes. Learning means facing squarely into our own ignorance, never a pretty sight.

The church is not a place to confirm our prejudices. It should be a place to redeem our prejudices. Seeing the light means letting go of some old ways of seeing our world. There will be no open eyes where there are no open minds. The last thing we may want to do at church is learn. Yet the word "disciple" means learner. If we want to follow, we have to keep learning.

But, opening our minds will not be enough. If we really want to see, we must be willing to open our hearts. Open minds without open hearts leads to arrogance and haughtiness. Closed hearts, "hardened hearts" as the Scripture calls it, cause us to hurt each other. Opening our hearts requires the spiritual discipline of taking other people seriously. We write people off too quickly. What becomes of you in God's eyes affects what becomes of me. We are in it together. We do not live in isolated places. How are we to meet each other? We can embrace or we can trample. Our lives connect. They overlap. The call of the gospel is to open our hearts. Nothing will open our eyes like looking into the eyes of another person.

In short, opening our hearts means caring. It does not mean loving those who love us, looking out for those who are always on our side. Caring means acting for the good of people you don't like, wrapping the wounds of people whose name you do not even know. We cannot open our eyes unless we are prepared to open our hearts.

Still, opening our minds and opening our hearts alone will not be enough to open our eyes. We have to find the courage to open our spirits. While we are not all religious people, we are all spiritual people. Above all else, being spiritual means that we cannot define ourselves by how many years we live or how much we have acquired or achieved. Each of us plays a single role in the human creation. No other person has your part in creation. There are no understudies. God only made one of you.

We often fear solitude—afraid that we will be lonely. Loneliness occurs not because we are alone but because we are empty. Opening our eyes, like Paul, means letting go of all the tugging and cajoling long enough to hear the inner call of God's spirit. While opening our minds may require learning and opening our hearts may require caring, opening our spirits requires the discipline of listening. We get too busy with our religion. Worship is about waiting and listening out for God. Prayer is a lot more about listening than talking. Growing in spirit is more about silence than chatter. We are consumed by noise, by the clamor, unable to listen. Growing in spirit means learning to treasure silence. We must learn to be together without talking. Learn to meet spirit to spirit. It will open our eyes.

So, as we leave the sanctuary, trying to see beyond our blindness, let us go with three brief lessons.

Lesson 1. We should spend a little time—perhaps three days, facing into our own blindness. We cannot see unless we are first prepared to bracket all our pronouncements and willing to see our own blindness. Draw aside from the distractions. Maybe it will require fasting or praying. It will certainly require facing up to the peculiar blindness that cripples our life. We must look into the prejudice, see the religious bigotry, see the resentment, and the fear that has captured our own lives and causes us to love life in the shadows.

Lesson 2. Opening our eyes is a discipline. The light hurts. We have to be willing to learn again, to take care of one another. Do something good for someone—out of the blue— no expectations. Nurture the life of spirit. Let go of the urge to control everything and everybody. Learn to treasure the silence.

Lesson 3. Finally, let us hear the word of the Lord. If we want to *see* light, we have to be willing to *be* light to somebody. We cannot be light to everybody. Our calling is more modest. It is to be light to somebody. We cannot be light to the world abstractly. We have to be light to a smaller world—a world that is closer to home.

So, today hear the gospel. Let's become light in somebody's world. If we want to see the light, we have to be willing to be light to somebody. There is somebody you know who feels like they are in the dark valley, consumed by the deep night—afraid. Embrace them, become light to them. Don't tell them about the light. Become light for them. Along the way, miracle of miracles, God will open our eyes.

Amen.

Simple Gifts*

Only a few years ago, *Forrest Gump* was the movie of the year. The movie could be described as a parable to simplicity. Its capacity to draw a crowd, no doubt, far outstripped its power as a parable. But, I suppose that we should claim the power of parables wherever we find them.

Forrest Gump was wrong of course. Life is not really like a box of chocolates. And though our culture may sometimes look and behave like something spawned by people with IQs of 75, most of you were born with the fortune, or the misfortune, of a far greater intellectual capacity. So, Forrest Gump will not likely endure as great literature. But the parable of Forrest Gump prompts me to speak of simplicity.

There are more powerful and poetic calls for simplicity than the story of Forest Gump. Thoreau, in *Walden II*, pronounced the essence of his social message in just two words: "Simplify, simplify."

You are coming to participate in a very competitive academic process at Mercer University, a process that will change the landscape of your life. You are entering an entirely new arena—a very different terrain, different voices, different appeals, different cries for your soul. A cauldron of complexity.

Your being invited to study here is a tribute to your ability, your persistence, and your discipline. You are among the best of the class. Forrest Gump would not have been admitted to Mercer. As you approach life in a university, it will not feel

---

*"Simple Gifts" was delivered to an entering first-year class of college students at Mercer University.

simple. You will be confronted with a welter of new people, challenging expectations, and oppressive freedom. Freedom will add to your complexity. People will stand in line to tell you what to do, where to live, what fraternity or sorority to join, how to behave, what to wear, and who to vote for. In coming to college, you are running headlong into a new kind of complexity.

The achievement of a measure of simplicity will not mean the absence of complexity. In our world, we are confronted by relentless tragedies in Iraq and Afghanistan, starvation in North Korea, caught between the emotions of rejecting the enemy and caring for the innocent, nonpolitical children, fear and distrust in the Middle East, chaos in many nations of Africa.

We also live in a tangled world. We live in a world where our best efforts to cope with racism and sexism remain woefully inadequate. We walk on streets that remain brutalized by crime. The fact is that your generation will face far greater difficulties than your parents' in addressing the awesome burdens of an aging population, environmental destruction, political stagnation, and a costly, out-of-control health-care system. Complexities. They are with us and they will be with you.

In the face of life's competing demands, our hope, our only hope, is to find a center, a place to stand, to find the learning and the integrity with which we can manage the web of responsibilities that cascade upon us. In the final analysis, that center will be about choosing to be somebody, to hold certain values, and to be going somewhere.

Finding a place to stand. That is a large part of the challenge of being in college. It is not that you will find a place and never move. Life is full of movement—shifting viewpoints, seeing the world through different lenses. During high school, family was the largest centering force in your life. You will not lose family, but there will be new moorings by which to measure your life. In these years at Mercer, you will find new relationships, some of which will become an important force in your life. You will discover a faculty mentor or a friend who will turn out to be a principal figure in shaping your life. But to live with simplicity means putting together an idea of yourself. Simplicity will mean laying claim to an idea of yourself by which you can measure your steps and judge your choices. College above all else, is about learning who you are and coming to understand your unique gift to the world.

Simplicity is both a gift and a discipline. It is a gift of learning to listen, of becoming at home with who you are and your own place in the world. It is a discipline because it requires practice and devotion. You cannot be everything to everybody. You cannot master every achievement. It requires the discipline to focus your energies, to climb a specific mountain rather than to fantasize about climbing every mountain.

As you undertake the discipline of simplicity, I offer you a few practical lessons with which to begin your collegiate journey.

1. Do today's work today. Tomorrow's work will take care of itself. The compounding of your work by delay, day after day, is the greatest threat to your ability to perform consistently at your best. Doing today's work tomorrow either leaves tomorrow's work undone or cheats the promise of today.

2. Preserve some time with yourself. The most important person you will get to know will be yourself. Solitude is an important gift to yourself. It should not be confused with

loneliness. Loneliness springs from being afraid. Solitude means coming to know yourself, to know your own thoughts, your own feelings. The gift of solitude will be among the most important steps you take toward becoming your own person.

3. Choose your priorities. In college you will be faced with doing many things. Choose a few. To decide means to cut away. Doing some things will mean choosing not to do some other things at all. You cannot lead every organization. You cannot participate in every club. You cannot attend every event. You cannot chase every dream. Choose your priorities and they will largely chart your course.

4. Learn to take yourself lightly. When my son went to college, I wrote him a long letter. I told him that I hoped he would make good mistakes. A good mistake is one that you can learn from and move beyond. I said to him what I would say to you. I do not worry about your making mistakes. I would worry far more about your never taking the kind of risks that would cause you to make mistakes. Learn to take yourself lightly enough that you can laugh at yourself. Laughter is a simple confession of our frailty.

5. Learn to listen. There is a time for speaking. But if you want to be heard and taken seriously when you speak, you must first learn to listen. Listening can take on many forms—watching, reading, hearing—really hearing what someone has to say. After you listen, then, make up your mind and speak.

6. Become a friend. Friendship means opening your inner self to someone else. Friendship is not a claim to stake. It is a gift to give. You had many friends in high school. You will make friends at Mercer that will be with you throughout your life. A few relationships will endure because they are bonded by the trust and respect and love that cannot be shattered by disagreement or even disappointments. Friendship is not a

goal to be sought. Friendship is an investment to make. Invest some time in being a friend.

7. Learn to change your mind. I was always attracted to the English philosopher, Bertrand Russell, because he radically changed his mind. Russell's critics often found his changing his mind to be a weakness. I say to you that is a strength. As you grow older, you will change your mind about some things, and that's good. Have the courage to change your mind.

8. You will from time to time be afraid—afraid of courses, afraid of professors, afraid even of the future. The ultimate remedy for fear is loving and caring. The ultimate remedy is to know that you are not finally alone. The usual reaction to fear is to shut ourselves off, to close the door. The real remedy runs the other direction. Open yourself, risk being present, risk giving and you will find the light called courage. Our option is not to live with or without fear. Our option is to live with or without courage.

Let me close with a story. During the eighteenth century, a small band of folks broke away from the Quakers in England and formed themselves into small communities called Shakers. I visited the remnants of a Shaker community in Kentucky several years back. The main teaching, as some of you may know, heralded the imminent return of Christ. Consequently, they were celibate and insisted upon living simple lives, not wanting to be entangled with worldly concerns, should Christ return during the night. (They even swept the floor of their meeting house after each evening service and they would hang the benches and the chairs on wall pegs so that their house would be in order if Christ should return during the night.)

We are almost amused by such Spartan, even bizarre behavior. Can you imagine such order in your residence hall? In reading the history of Mercer, I was intrigued by the lifestyle of the students of Mercer's early years in the 1830s. School opened every morning at sunrise with the reading of Scripture and prayer. Students then engaged in physical exercises. Scholastic exercises were begun shortly thereafter and except for lunch, were continued until two hours before sundown, at which time the students went to their labors on the farm. No BMWs allowed.

But back to the Shakers. The American composer, Aaron Copland, inspired by folk tunes and simple stories, incorporated a Shaker hymn tune into his great *Appalachian Spring*, a ballet which Martha Graham choreographed and which she and her ballet group premiered in 1944 in Washington, at the Library of Congress. Today, *Appalachian Spring* is frequently performed in concert halls throughout the world.

The Shaker hymn tune originally accompanied the lyrics known as "Simple Gifts." Listen to the words of the first verse and the refrain.

'Tis the gift to be simple, 'tis the gift to be free
'Tis the gift to come down where we ought to be.
And when we find ourselves in the place just right,
'Twill be the valley of love and delight.

(Refrain)
    When true simplicity is gain'd,
    To bow and to bend we shan't be ashamed.
    To turn, turn will be our delight,
    'Till by turning, turning we come round right.

As you consider your years of college, I want to encourage within you a measure of simplicity. All of you are bright and gifted students. You can learn to solve problems and to chart new alternatives in a difficult and challenging world. But it will require the simplicity of discipline. Learning, caring, relating. These are the simple gifts.

This university will call you to rigorous hard work. We will foster your imagination, encourage you to be creative, to probe the boundaries of what you have thought and believed before. But most of all we will believe in you, and our calling is to build within you the courage to believe in yourself. Learn with discipline. Live with integrity. Embrace one another with friendship and joy. These are the simple gifts that will transform your college career into a journey that will change the story of your life.

The Children of Cain

We are violent people. Violence runs deep in our soul, erupting painfully and tragically in our daily lives together. Violence is not simply a phenomenon of 9/11 or Iraq. It is not a phenomenon of Atlanta or New York or Sarajevo or Kabul. It is not a tragedy spawned by Hitler or Stalin, by North Korea or Palestinians. Blame is indeed a response that falls too easily from our lips. Blame is a way of escape.

In all candor, violence is often the human way of being together. We are people who are determined to make our own way, to build our own cities, to establish our own hierarchies, and to assert our own power. Over and over, we commit violence trying to have our own way. We are the children of Cain. We, like Cain, soothe ourselves saying, "Why, God, are you looking at me?" I'm just sitting here watching it on television. I'm not out there beating or looting or burning. Why look at me?

Reverberating within us is the unspoken realization that we are violent people. We usually look for more civilized ways to burn and pillage and kill. Yet, when we can no longer contain our rage or hold back our flood of fear, we turn to wanton and tragic destruction.

Our human civilization continues to be defined more by violence than by compassion. Rage arises in all of us—white and black, rich and poor, learned and illiterate. We usually cover our rage with a thin veil of propriety. But rage lies deeply lodged in our character. We are profoundly violent people. We are the children of Cain. We are sustained and protected by violence and we often pursue our national goals in violent ways.

And when violence erupts, the only resource to which we know to turn is more violence. We send out the troops. We put on riot gear and we take to the streets to establish order. Strangely, both order and disorder claim the tools of violence. Our violence will outdo your violence and order will prevail. Violence is the human way.

The stories of Genesis could teach us that violence belongs to the order of original sin. There is no good violence. Killing Abel is our way of establishing our priority, of making our sacrifice acceptable, or wanting to make sure that we are favored.

The violence of Columbine, Waco, Oklahoma City, New York City stuns us. It is more like running into a signpost than seeing one. In the face of tragedy, we become silent, not knowing quite what to say. In our time, the universality of violence has become so vivid and naked. The system, the culture, the nation—permeated with violence.

- The violence of policemen—no argument about their violent actions, only whether it was "appropriate."
- The bitterness of a victim—not only the victim of a policeman's baton but a victim of his own anger and emptiness.
- The violence of hopeless and helpless people, burning and looting, making their own despair into a despair for others.
- The despair of a family whose truck-driver son drove into the wrong place, beaten violently by people who did not even know him, much less hate him.

Violence, violence, all is violence. It leaves us empty. I want us to recognize that violence is not far from our own steps. Violence is not 3,000 miles away in L.A., not 10,000 miles away in the Middle East, not even 100 miles away in Atlanta.

Violence is our way of being together. It comes in many shades. It wears many faces. We destroy Abel in countless ways—the violence of power, the violence of economic peril, the violence of uniformity, the violence of sexuality, the violence of silence. On and on we could go.

Look at our way of life together.

The violence of power. Violence is power out of control—whether the power of splitting atoms in a nuclear plant or the power of position in your fraternity, or BSU, or the power of authority in administration or the power of teaching. Violence may use guns or knives or violence may use words and decisions.

Look at our way of life together. The violence of sexuality is everywhere present. Sexual abuse victimizes more people than were victims in south central L.A. Child abuse, spouse abuse, rape—using sex to control. Much of people's sexual behavior violates the independence and selfhood of another person.

Look at our way of life together. The violence of economic peril. We cannot sustain democracy where economic progress ignores poverty, joblessness, and economic hopelessness. We have tolerated, if not fostered, an economic condition that places too many people in a kind of jeopardy that breeds gang warfare and street violence. If we ignore economic injustice, it will finally burn democracy to the ground.

Look at our way of life together. The violence of uniformity—forcing others to be like us, to think as we think, to believe as we believe. Different color, different language, different beliefs are a threat. So we cast people out and we wonder why they gather in gangs.

Look at our way of life together. Perhaps none is more deceiving than the violence of silence. We have stood by, remained quiet, avoided the issues. We cannot recover our national integrity or maintain personal or institutional integrity unless we speak. Genuine speaking always includes listening. We have lots of folks shouting past each other with self-righteous indignation. The path of hope lies neither in speaking that has no room for listening, nor in silence that has no room for speaking. As a society and as individuals, we have tolerated abuse and neglect until we have become perpetuators of violence.

We are Cain's children. We can hardly bear for others to gain the approval for which we long. So we, like Cain, find a hundred different ways to dispose of Abel. We diminish, dismiss, and destroy. We keep women in their place. We classify one another by race and knowledge and rank. We try to climb ahead of the rest, establishing our strength even by assuring the weakness of somebody else. We are the descendants of Cain, putting each other down, scoffing at one another's mistakes, taking the low ground of moral and intellectual superiority.

The truth is that violence arises from souls that are wrenched by fear and anger. Fear and anger breed the malice and brutality that consumes us.

Like Cain, we hurt people because we are afraid—afraid that we will be hurt, afraid that our frail and fragile hold on life will be lost—afraid that we will lose our grip and fall into the abyss.

Like Cain, we hurt people because we are angry—angered by isolation and abandonment, angered by abuse and neglect—so angry that we strike out, giving mute but visible testimony to our inner hurt.

Fear and anger are embedded deep within us. But hear this word. Fear will not be arrested by force or the show of strength. We must somehow learn better. Fear will not be stemmed by the dispatch of troops or the pronouncements of law and order. Fear will abate and the anger will subside only when we discover and commit to a new way of being together. If we are to escape the grips of violence, it will not be because we have grown stronger; it will only be because we have grown wiser.

And where is wisdom for a violent people? How are we to deal with the violence in L.A. and in our own souls? The fact is that our eggshell world is broken to pieces—shattered and lying in crumbles and smoldering ashes.

What are we to do with the pieces?

I confess to you that the only place I know to turn for a clue is the presence and the voice of Jesus—himself both victim of and victor over human violence. Jesus faced violence not as an abstract, impersonal experience, not as a philosopher or a teacher. He felt violence as a dreadful, devastating, shattering, avalanche coming into his own life.

Violence visited Jesus in the Garden where he was arrested in the presence of his disciples. Roman soldiers with their swords and their paraphernalia of war marched into the Garden of Prayer—violating the night with the weapons of conflict.

Yet, the disciples had not learned. We seem never to learn. Peter, the most swashbuckling of all the disciples, confronted violence with violence. That is our way. He drew the sword, cut off the ear of the approaching soldier—yielding violence for violence. It is our way—meeting violence head on, holding our ground, taking on the enemy.

What are we to do with the pieces?

If Jesus is our clue, listen to his way.

1. First, we have to pick up the ear and put it back on. Violence will never cure violence. And there is no easy or shortcut way to pick up the pieces. But, that is what we must do. We have to rebuild what our violence has destroyed. We have to put the ear back. We have to heal the wounds of violence. We may have to suture it. It will leave scars. We have to go to the rubble and rake up the debris. We have to rebuild the building, equip the storefronts, place goods back on the shelves.

We ought to tax ourselves, sacrifice ourselves, invest ourselves in rebuilding from the ashes. It is not enough to say "I'm sorry" and to shake our heads in disbelief. In short, our struggle must be to find ways to redeem the violence. We have to put the ear back on. We must find the wisdom not to respond to violence with violence, but with careful, concerted, constructive acts of redemption.

We need to invest and repair, until South Central L.A. looks better, feels better, and is better than it has ever been. And we must do it here in Macon, in our own neighborhoods. In the place of wreckage, our obligation is to bring hope. Where there are ashes, our obligation is to build stores and to rescue people in pain.

2. Second, we must find concrete and specific ways of responding to violence with compassion. If Jesus is our clue, there is only one cure to rage. That cure is holy, deliberate, willful caring. Jesus says to us that love is the only way out of the descending spiral of hatred. Love, which sounds so weak, is the only power strong enough to overcome fear and eradicate rage. Hatred can never drive out hatred. Only love will do that. Violence can never cure violence. Only love will do that.

It is a hard word because it has not been our way. Our way is to suppress violence with violence. The way of Jesus sounds so foolish. It is the gospel. Love casts out fear.

3. A final word. Jesus met violence with forgiveness. Simple forgiveness. You and I have designed our own special brand of forgiveness—a brand of forgiveness that breaks and cripples the one being forgiven. "Oh, I'll forgive you this time, but you had better never let it happen again."

We should not confuse our forgiveness with forgetting. You have heard it, "Oh, just forget it." Forgiveness rarely means to forget. It more likely means to remember. Forgiveness means to remember the violence, to remember L.A., to remember Watts, to remember Birmingham and Selma and New York—and to live beyond those tragedies. Living beyond them means not letting our lives or our relationships be defined by those tragedies.

Beyond revenge, forgiveness means to embrace, to lift each other up, to lift up even our enemies. It means to walk beyond the desolation together because we see in one another the face of God. You may have to look hard, but God is there. If Jesus is our clue, we must meet violence with forgiveness.

Hear the word from God. We are all victims—victims of fear, victims of anger. And out of that fear has grown the ravages of violence. The responsibility for that violence does not rest with African Americans, or Native Americans, or Asian Americans, or Anglo-Saxon Americans. The responsibility rests with how you and I choose to live together— guided more by fear than by love.

Jesus lived out for us the hope of breaking the boundaries of fear, of setting us free from fear—free to be together in a new way.

Free to reach out
Free to lift up
Free to give hope

Free to love
Free to forgive

Jesus calls on you and me to throw down the swords of violence, to take up the tools of hope. We, like Cain, are the children of violence.

We murder
We maim
We neglect
We harass
We intimidate
We abuse
We sit silent

Yet, we, like Cain, bear the mark of God. And that mark means that God is with us and will not leave our side. God will not leave the side of the neglected or those who neglect. God will not leave the side of the abused or those who abuse, the victim or the victor. God will not leave the side of the violent or the violated.

And God's word in Jesus is to bring us together in a new way—picking up the pieces, confronting rage with compassion, meeting violence with forgiveness, setting us free to live as the people of God.

What do we do with the violence?

We confess that we are like Cain, our brother—profane, angry, afraid, putting our brother to the ground.

And we listen to the gospel. The word of the gospel for us today is to let go of our fear. Pick up the pieces. Heal the wounds. Build it back. And God will make us into a new nation. We too can become the people of God, a kingdom of priests, free to forgive and free to love. Then we can hear the faint echoes of Martin Luther King, Jr.:

> Free at last!
> Free at last!
> Thank God Almighty,
> we are Free at last.

Amen.